MOTIVATE
THE
UNMOTIVATED

A PROVEN SYSTEM FOR SUSTAINABLE MOTIVATION

BY MATT GRANADOS

Motivate the Unmotivated: A Proven System for Sustainable Motivation

RHG Media Productions
25495 Southwick Drive #103
Hayward, CA 94544.

ISBN 978-1735099712 (paperback)
ISBN 978-1735099729 (hardcover)

Visit us on line at www.RHG/MediaProductions or www.sherylglick.com

Printed in the United States of America.

DEDICATION

When the publisher asked me to write a short message for the dedication, I found it hard to keep it short. I have been blessed with connecting with individuals all over the world who have poured into me through their knowledge and experience.

The single most important person I must dedicate this book to is the one person who motivates me more than anyone on this planet. That is my wife, Maria. Outside of her being an amazing partner and mom, her presence and who she is as a person makes me (and anyone she is around) want to be a better version of themselves. I am dedicating this book primarily to her as without her support, help, and guidance I would have never completed this book.

Second, I would like to dedicate this to the rest of my immediate family. My kids Natalie and Zach have taught me so much as a father. My siblings have set bars high enough for me to have to reach and are always willing to push/support me as I reach for them. And I would like to dedicate this to my parents, who have ALWAYS supported me even when I was a mess. Outside of constant love from both, my mom has instilled drive and grit into me and my dad has been an example of a man who I continuously strive to be like.

And finally, I need to dedicate this book to the single most influential experience of my life.

At 15 I went to a youth program that Maria and I both continue to be a part of today. To this date, I have dedicated nearly all my success in both my personal life and professional life to Eagle University. I would urge anyone who knows someone between the ages of 15-24 years old to find a way to get those young people to this program. You can reach out to us directly or go to their website (www.EagleUniversity.org). I tell you this because of all I received from it, and I truly believe it would be a disservice to others if I did not introduce it to anyone who cared about a student in that age range!

At this program, I learned life lessons that to this day are still bearing fruit. This is when I was first introduced to the concept of mentors along with countless other life skills that I would never have learned in traditional schooling. The mentors I met at that program have become life-long friends and some business partners.

From 15 years old to today, there have been many other mentors (you know who you are) who have helped shape me and sharpen me as an individual in all areas of my life. This book is dedicated to you, too. This book was not created because of who I am, it was made possible by those who have poured into me throughout the years. So, I thank each and every one of you who has helped me along the way.

TABLE OF CONTENTS

CHAPTER 1
VALUE IS THE KEY TO LIFE
GET THE CAR MOVING

How do you motivate the unmotivated? If you chose to read this book, one of two things are probably happening in your life. For some, maybe both of the following are happening at the same time. You picked this book up because you are responsible for motivating either yourself or others to reach an end goal. Maybe you have someone in your life—could be a group, could be an individual, could be you—who is just flat out unmotivated, and you're at a loss for what to do about it.

Regardless of which you're dealing with, this book will break down the big ideas and show you exactly how to motivate the unmotivated effectively...no matter how unmotivated they might be. But why wait until the end for the big reveal? Why not just give you the answer right here, in the first chapter?

Editors and publishers suggested that I should not do this. They thought that if I gave you the answer right away, you wouldn't keep reading. As you read through this book, you will notice that my tactics and way of doing things are not at all conventional.

But why would an author just hand over the answer to you in the first few pages? The logic is simpler than you might think. A mentor of mine, Steven J. Anderson (Founder of Total Patients Services Institute & Co-Founder of Crown Council), has drilled it into my head since I was a teenager. No matter what topic he would teach or what strategy he would suggest, he would always tell me, "There is a difference between knowing and doing!"

I will give you the secret to motivating the unmotivated shortly, and then I will let you decide if you would like to take the step past just "knowing" and actually learn the "doing" by reading the rest of this book. There are many times as humans when we know what we should do but we end up doing something we shouldn't. Knowledge is nothing without the ability to properly act on it.

The answer to motivating the unmotivated is simple, and this book will give it to you. Each chapter will dive into the Motivation Formula and its components to give you applicable, implementable takeaways for how to boost motivation in all areas of your life...as well as the lives of others.

I promise you; this book will make you think differently about how you interact with individuals and yourself. Even the few concepts that you may have heard before and the ones you may already practice will be seen in a different light. I will guide you on how to implement these practices effectively and positively in your everyday life.

So, what is the solution to motivating the unmotivated? First, we need to dive into the reasons why a person would be unmotivated. We will also explore the inspiration and success that come when you do feel motivated.

A person who is unmotivated has what we might describe as a weakened Motivation Synapse between their actions and outcomes. It is almost as if the unmotivated are unable to connect their actions with the probable outcomes until they see them play out, whereas motivated individuals can connect their current actions with the end result before it happens and, therefore, keep pushing themselves in order to make that next result happen. As a result of this weakened synapse, unmotivated people tend to have tunnel vision. They focus entirely on the actions or tasks they are doing right now. It is like the concepts of cause and effect have no correlation but rather are two independent, inevitable events.

But remember, being unmotivated is not a personality trait; it is a current state of mind.

It appears that unmotivated individuals sit somewhere between lazy and unaware. Lazy is a choice, and it is usually our default way to describe people who are unmotivated. However, most unmotivated people are this way not because they are lazy, but rather because of a lack of awareness. Both can be corrected by following the techniques in this book. In order to change this state of mind and motivate the unmotivated, we need to strengthen this synapse between actions and outcomes. We can do this by bringing value to the unmotivated individual's actions. We help them, take the time to listen to them, and understand what it is they value. So, essentially, we ask questions.

Sounds simple enough, right? But how does this Motivation Synapse work? A synapse, by definition, is "a junction between two nerve cells, consisting of a minute gap across which impulses pass by diffusion of a neurotransmitter."[1] This connection enables neurotransmitters to pass messages between neurons. However, they can weaken over time. With the Motivation Synapse, the junction is between action and outcome, and it can be weakened or strengthened depending on how actively you manage your motivation levels. A weakening synapse between action and outcome does not just happen to a select group of people. In fact, it has probably

---

[1] "Synapse," Lexico, Oxford, http://www.lexico.com/en/definition/synapse.

happened to all of us. At some point in our life we will, or have, all been unmotivated in some way, shape, or form.

The weakening of the Motivation Synapse can occur on its own, because of the individual's mindset, or it can occur because of an outside source or experience. We just end up going through the motions, with little regard for the future. When intentionality starts to drift away, no matter what caused it to happen, it tends to reflect our lack of understanding of the purpose of the tasks we are doing.

With, motivating the unmotivated boils down to asking the right questions in order to help the unmotivated understand and connect their purpose with their tasks. In doing that, you will strengthen the synapse between action and outcome!

Well, you now have the simple answer to why people are unmotivated and what to do to motivate the unmotivated. But remember, knowledge is worthless without application. In this book, you will find individual sections that provide simple strategies for you to use in order to implement this knowledge in your life and relationships.

I hope you are excited to jump into this book, turn the page, and come on this journey with me. This quest has been shaped by experience, as well as by other individuals who are undoubtedly way smarter than me. I have learned how to motivate the unmotivated in all areas of my life, with all types of people, and received consistent results using the techniques detailed in this book.

I will ask you to read this book from two different perspectives—both as motivator and as motivatee. Or even better, I suggest re-reading it multiple times while referring to different roles and relationships in your life. Some readers will see themselves as the one doing the motivating. They might have people responding to them or people they manage. That is fine, and you will get more information on your team out of this book than any other generic book on motivation.

What I would challenge you to do is not to forget the second, self-reflective lens to look through, which will allow you to see yourself needing motivation as well. We all like to say that we are motivated—and I am not doubting that you are—but as you read this book, think about how you are being received by others. Are you as motivated as they think you are, more, or less?

The goal of this book is not to share complex, abstract theories that give you the "why" but not the "how" of motivation. Rather, my aim is to introduce motivational concepts that are impactful, simplify them as much as possible, and give you action steps for how you can apply them to your life.

There are millions of self-help books on store shelves, some of which are general in nature and others that are extremely targeted. This book focuses on the relationships between two people. Here's a quick test to see if it's a good fit for you. I want you to go through the list below and see if it includes any relationships in your life where you'd like to see the other person a bit more motivated:

Boss - Employee - Team - Manager - Customer - Parent - Child - Sibling - Spouse - Friend - Pet (seriously, it works) - Any human at all

So yes, the list above is exhaustive, and that's intentional. Still, this system works. It isn't a quick-fix course on how to manipulate people. I'm not going to teach you tricks to get inside other people's heads and change who they are. I will, however, teach you a proven system and belief structure that when earnestly applied, works 100 percent of the time.

The first step is to think about the single most unmotivated person in your life. This individual is experiencing a weakened Motivation Synapse between their actions and outcomes. It may seem like they live one day at a time and have no idea tomorrow is coming. Or, maybe they just don't care and are struggling in more ways than one. Either way, they can be anywhere on the unmotivated scale, from consciously lazy to completely unaware. Now, like I said, think about someone you would like to motivate and use these suggestions with to help get the ball rolling with them.

Who would you most like to see become more motivated? Who would have the most significant impact on your life if you could fundamentally change their level of motivation? Once you have that person in mind, instead of embarrassing them by writing out their name in this book, let us introduce you to our main character.

Meet Unmo. This is the character we'll use as your personal case study throughout the rest of the book. While you know the names of people in your life who might be experiencing this unmotivated mindset. Remember, unmotivated is not a characteristic, it is a mindset. For the people in your life who have this mindset of unmotivated, we'll refer to them all in the coming chapters as "Unmo." If you cannot think of the one person in your life, think of someone who could use help correcting this unmotivated mindset. We all have a few Unmos in our life and we have all been Unmo at some point in our life so feel free to focus on one specific Unmo throughout the whole book or pick different Unmos for different chapters. Alright, let's get started.

CHAPTER 2
THE HARDEST PERSON
I EVER NEEDED TO MOTIVATE
The Scariest Sight to See

The heartbeat tells the story of life.

When you hear the term "flatline," you probably think of someone lying in a hospital bed, covered in wires and tubes, surrounded by weeping family members. In the background, a doctor is looking at an EKG monitor that reflects no sign of life. This isn't a pleasant image, but it's an accurate one—the heartbeat tells the story of life, and when there's no heartbeat, we know that life is gone.

While this might be the first visual your mind creates, the lessons it shows can be repeated in virtually any area of life. "Life" isn't limited to the biological mechanism of a heart beating; it involves hope and disappointment, love, and loss, joy, and pain. These are all necessary ingredients in life. No matter who you are, you'll experience these feelings many times in a variety of ways until the day you die.

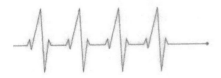 A heartbeat is an excellent visual representation of the ebb and flow of life. There is an awfully specific and intentional pattern as the heart contracts and releases when properly circulating blood throughout the body. When that rhythm is shown on an EKG, it looks like this: up and down, up, and down.

As I've grown older, I'm continually amazed at how this pattern mirrors life with all of its ups and downs. I want to zoom in on one of these beats that I have termed my "Heartbeat" and show you how this design has shown up in my own life.

(A) In 2008, I graduated from college and felt like the world was my oyster. I had just secured an internship working for one of the wealthiest individuals in the world, and I pictured my career unfolding like a red carpet in front of me. I was in school to go into the hospitality industry, and my dream was to own a casino. I had a passion for it, and the effort I put into my internship demonstrated that commitment.

(B) I was successful throughout this internship and at the end received job offers to work at virtually any property in the world. I sat down with a mentor of mine who was *the* top person in the casino industry—the man who essentially built Las Vegas. I wanted to get his advice regarding the next steps in my career path and how I should move forward. I walked into the conversation full of excitement, knowing I'd given my all up to this point and knowing my work reflected that.

That was when the bottom dropped out. He looked me in the eye and said, "Matt, you're not a good fit for the casino industry. This isn't where you should be."

It felt like a dagger to the heart. If you had spent your entire life dreaming of being a professional basketball player, worked your butt off every day, gone to all the right training camps, and been mentored by experts every step of the way, think about where your mind would be if you got a chance to sit down and chat with Michael Jordan. Now think about how you'd feel if he said you really shouldn't be playing basketball. I was crushed.

(C) I spent a lot of time reflecting on my life over the next few weeks, which is when I made a critical discovery. The casino industry itself had never been the attraction for me—the thought of the freedom I would experience if I *owned* a casino had always been the appeal. I realized I'd never actually been passionate about casinos, and I didn't have to be in the gaming industry to own my own business.

I dug deep into my skill sets and passions, dividing my interests and talents into the things I loved and the things I tolerated. One thing that stood out above everything else was the joy I experienced when making a sale, and I knew that whatever I did next it needed to revolve around this core concept. It wasn't until years later, as you will see later in this book, that I was able to recognize this fatal mistake I was making. I was full throttle towards my passions but in no way did I recognize, understand, or leverage my purpose. If I knew to put purpose over passions, this story would have been way less painful for me.

At the ripe young age of twenty-three, with the help of two amazing mentors turned business partners, I moved to Atlanta and started my own business. Within a year, I had generated over a million dollars in sales and the company was a multimillion-dollar organization. For the next four years, we experienced unprecedented growth and life was great. I had the business I always wanted, more money than I needed, and was engaged to a woman with whom I wanted to share my life.

(D) As I was preparing my taxes in March 2014, I realized that my cash didn't match up with my books. The company had an awesome year with several million in sales, so I called my accountant and asked for an explanation. He calmly explained that the discrepancy wasn't an issue because I had over six figures tied up in inventory.

His reassurance put me at ease and allowed me to sleep that night. When I woke up the next morning, I went straight to the warehouse to count the inventory and confirm the news for myself. When I saw what was left, I knew my worst fears had been realized. The merchandise wasn't there. I investigated and found that a group of my sales reps had worked together to "mismanage" and embezzle the missing six figure worth of inventory, selling it for cash on the side. However, I had no real proof of it happening and no viable way to recoup the lost inventory. Due to my inexperience as an entrepreneur, I lacked the necessary systems to identify this issue in a timely manner, so by the time I discovered it the corruption had spread throughout the company.

I was young and, although street smart, I was relatively uneducated in entrepreneurial life lessons. I hadn't realized how terribly managed my inventory was. Although the company had bulletproof sales systems, my operations and inventory management systems left a lot to be desired.

This was a massive blow to my self-esteem. From the outside, I looked like a complete success. On the inside, I felt cheated, stupid, worthless, and a total failure. At this point, I was twenty-six and owned a multimillion-dollar business thought to be extremely profitable, but, it was so mismanaged that I was hemorrhaging cash. I felt like a famous athlete who went broke a year after signing a multimillion-dollar contract. I sat back and took stock of my life, comforting myself with the knowledge that at least I had my health, peace of mind, and my fiancée. I could recover. It was going to be okay.

(E) I'd always been continually active and played sports throughout school, but when I started my business, work took over and my health took a backseat. A mentor had advised me that each year, on my birthday, I should get a physical to ensure that I still had a clean bill of health. A few weeks after I discovered the embezzlement, I went to my annual appointment and received a less than perfect report for the first time in my life. It wasn't anything major, but the amount of stress I was experiencing on a day-to-day basis was what most people experience at their peak stress level. I was operating at a constant level of stress and just considered it my new norm. The bottom line is that no one's body can withstand that constant strain without eventually shutting down.

I went out to the car and talked myself through things again. I had just had a significant setback in business, but that was okay; it was a good lesson learned, and I could recover. I wasn't in the greatest shape ever, but I could fix that. I focused on my fiancée, the life we were going to build together, and my peace of mind.

(F) The next morning, I woke up and checked my finances. For the first time in my life, there were zeroes across all my accounts. Nothing was in the red; it was simply all gone. That was one of the eeriest sights I've ever seen, one that I will never forget. The fallout from the embezzlement fiasco had drained my bank accounts, and I was too ashamed and embarrassed to tell anyone. I couldn't even mention it to my fiancée. At this point, she was all I had left, and I didn't want to feel more like a loser by taking another step down in her mind.

I went on a retreat to my stomping grounds in Pennsylvania with the hope of clearing my head. I didn't have a real relationship with God at this point, but I remembered begging him for help. I didn't know what was happening, where I was in life, or how to recover. I was completely lost.

I flew back to Atlanta, determined to take control of my life. My fiancée and I were days away from leaving for a much-needed vacation in Greece. I remember thinking how grateful I was that everything had already been paid for. This would be an excellent opportunity to reset, reconnect with my fiancée, and get my feet back under me. I started to psych myself up for the trip, just like I would before a big game in high school. This was where I'd turn a corner.

When I arrived home on the day before we were supposed to leave for our trip, my fiancée brought me her ring and told me it was over. She couldn't handle the relationship anymore. At the time, I was so blind to how hard it must have been for her to be in an empty relationship. Looking back, I can see why I felt I had nothing to offer her. I was out of money. From a health perspective, I was dying faster than I was living. And I didn't have any peace of mind.

(G) I couldn't get a refund for my trip, so I went to Greece by myself. At this point, I was drifting and just felt a desperate need to get away. Despite my apprehensions, I enjoyed myself. I had the chance to get out of my environment, exercise, meet new people, and take a break from a world I felt was rapidly disintegrating. For a moment, things felt semi-normal. Unfortunately, the trip came to an end, and I had to leave my worry-free vacation.

(H) I didn't realize how hard it would be to return to an empty house. All the momentum I had gained on my trip instantly vanished; I felt like the wind had been taken out of my sails. Everything was a reminder of the long list of things that had gone wrong. The positive side of things was that there wasn't much left to lose. Things didn't get any lower, but my day-to-day was empty and lifeless, like I couldn't gain any traction. I felt like I was just existing.

(I) I tried hard, but every time I had a small victory, (J) it was immediately followed by a downturn. These defeats weren't huge, objectively speaking, but I was so hypersensitive at that point that everything felt like a blow. I started to avoid getting my hopes up, because it almost always meant disappointment was soon to follow. It was amazing how blind I was to the realities of my own life. My employees stole from me, my fiancée left me, and I eventually found out that there was someone else on the side. My health was diminishing, and there was absolutely no growth in my life. I was the definition of lost!

(K) In the second quarter of 2014, I volunteered with a youth leadership program, Eagle University (www.eagleuniversity.org), as a guest speaker. I had been a part of this program for a decade, first as a student and later as a mentor. I had agreed to speak months prior before everything went south. While I didn't feel like I had anything to offer, I believed in following through with my commitments. Truth be told, I didn't even think I deserved to be there with my suitcase full of recent failures.

I showed up and gave it everything I had, expecting nothing in return. However, the act of serving others when I felt like I had nothing was a turning point in my life, transforming me in a way I couldn't have possibly imagined. I met Maria, who I knew instantly when I met her, that she would be someone who I could spend the rest of my life with. I was in a rough spot but even through the darkness, I could see what an amazing individual she was and I am blessed to have her as my wife and perfect match. In the months that followed, my life experienced a drastic change. Through all of this, I found my wife, found God, completed an Ironman triathlon, and reinvented my business. Prior to all this falling apart, I would have claimed to be living a fulfilled life but at this moment, I truly felt fulfilled I felt like I had become a winner again.

That's when the biggest change hit me: it was a simple, but profound, realization. It was a question I randomly heard in my head, and before I even knew the answer, I understood why my life had fallen apart. The question that kept eating away at me was simply: "When was the last time you grew?" It stopped me in my tracks.

I had stopped growing myself. I was so busy working on my business, my relationship, and my investments that I'd forgotten about *myself*. Stephen Covey, in his landmark book *the 7 Habits of Highly Effective People*, talks about the importance of sharpening your ax. He uses the example of a woodcutter who never stops whacking trees: as time goes on, he works harder and harder but gets less done. His blade has gotten dull. Meanwhile, another woodcutter stops after every tree, sits down with a file, and takes five minutes just to work on recovering for the next project.

I knew I needed to get myself back, and that proved to be my most significant challenge. Motivating others when life's good is easy—you can distance yourself from the struggles and failures they're experiencing and choose to focus on the positive. When you're emotionally destroyed, you see life very differently. Waking up every day with no excitement, no drive, and no feeling of purpose made it hard to motivate myself and impossible to motivate others.

As I reflected on everything that had brought me to this point, I realized that the pattern of my life looked *exactly* like a heartbeat.

A – Graduated college, started a dream internship
B – Had my dreams shattered by an expert mentor
C – Recovered, started a business, earned millions
D – Massive employee embezzlement
E – Doctor gave me a bad bill of health
F – Lost all my money, fiancée walked out on me

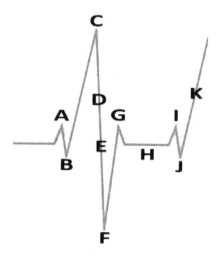

G – Went to Greece and actually enjoyed myself
H – Plateaued: no big successes, no big failures
I – Started to get small victories
J – Victories were immediately followed by defeats
K – Learned to give back to others, realized I needed to invest in 4 specific areas in my life that you will read about later in the book called the 4 Vital Signs of Fulfillment.

"What happened?" That was the one question that was going through my head, on repeat, for months. I'd always been very self-confident: I had the belief that I was able to do anything and had the résumé to back it up. However, even with all of that, I'd managed to fall flat on my face in every area of my life.

This story is important because I'm not describing a freak accident or a surprise occurrence that came out of nowhere. It *felt* like it came out of nowhere—but only because I was looking in all the wrong places.

The incidents described in D–F above all came about because of my own choices. My employees stole from me because I gave them an opportunity to do so, but even more than that, I'd created such a worthless culture in my business that they felt as if they deserved it. My doctor told me that I wasn't healthy because of how I had lived my life over the last year.

Whenever I share my story, I typically get a lot of sympathy, especially when I tell the part about my ex-fiancée walking out on me. Listen, it was rough. Loyalty is my primary core value, so I find dealing with any infidelity particularly tough. I have a lot of reasons to blame her, and it would probably be easier for me to put the death of the relationship exclusively on her, but in reality, it was an unhealthy relationship. We never argued, which some would consider a sign of health. Yet that couldn't be further from the truth. If there is no disagreement in a relationship, either someone doesn't care, or someone is getting bullied. In our case, it was a little bit of both: I was a bulldozer without even realizing it, and at some point, she stopped caring. I'm not always an easy person to be with. My ex-fiancée did what she needed to do for herself at the time.

As painful and confusing as this whole time in my life was, if I had to go through it again to guarantee I would get to be with Maria and live the life we have, I'd do it willingly. Heck, I'd do it a few times over.

The most important lesson I hope you take from this chapter is how most of the "downs" in my life can all be traced to prior actions and decisions I made. Occasionally, we encounter devastating blows in life that come out of nowhere, but most of the time we hold at least some part of the blame...and oftentimes most of it.

Rather than being a discouraging reality, this should give us hope. If we are the ones responsible for how we react to the downturns in our life, that means we can prevent them by making better choices in the future.

The foundation of motivating others is a stable you. Making the right choices, investing in yourself, and mastering the art of motivation by being able to pick yourself up when you feel worthless and hopeless—these form the groundwork for motivating others.

As you work through the rest of the book, you'll have the temptation to jump straight to the "them" part of the formula. I want you to resist this urge. Instead, focus on developing the habit of stopping and mentally applying these lessons to yourself before you begin evaluating others.

CHAPTER 3
HERE'S HOW IT WORKS
Simple and Effective

There's nothing conventional about motivating the unmotivated. Each relationship is completely unique; in fact, you might even have different relationships with the same person. If you work in a family business, for example, your brother-in-law might be your co-worker, and each of those roles requires a different way of relating to him. In every interpersonal relationship, there is a "motivator" (the person doing the motivating) and a "motivatee" (the one being motivated), but this is not to say that these roles don't flip flop. The primary goal of this book is to equip you to be an effective motivator, but one of the side effects of learning this system is that you'll be able to receive motivation more effectively from positive people in your life—and that's always a good thing.

Let's jump into Motivation 101.

Motivation 101

Motivation suffers from more than its fair share of myths. Here are two of the ones I hear most often:

- You can't motivate everyone.
- You can't motivate people unless they want to be motivated.

Two opposing truths populate the pages of this book:

- Everyone can be motivated.
- If you intentionally implement the principles in this book, *you* can motivate anyone.

Motivation is a process, not an event. Naturally, all of us are born with desires so everyone is driven by something, but it often takes getting to know a person before you discover what that is. The first step in that process, and easiest way for this to become sustainable is caring about someone. This allows you to create an environment where people not only feel safe sharing, they will *want* to tell you about themselves because they know you care.

A galvanizing factor in someone's life is called a "motivating proposition," or "M-Prop," as I like to refer to it. This is a term that might sound familiar to you, especially if you have a background in marketing, because it's derived from the concept of a "value proposition." A value proposition is an innovation, service, or feature intended to make a company or product attractive to customers. Although the term changes slightly for our purposes, the core concept is precisely the same: when someone sees the benefit and value of acting a different way, he or she will change whatever is needed to obtain that value.

We can use a simple illustration from nature. Plant life is incredibly varied, just like people are. Although plants have an incredibly diverse range of needs, at their very core they all have the same motivational factor: sunlight. From the smallest blade of grass to the giant sequoia tree, each plant is driven upward as it reaches for that vital solar energy. If you've ever seen plants weave their way through a tumultuous series of obstacles to reach the sunlight, you can easily understand how the right catalyst will always drive living beings to overcome any obstacle.

When it comes to motivating people, one core concept we need to understand is that there are always two parties involved. This is called the **Two-Party System of Motivation**, and this system can be just as productive, or destructive, as its political reference. I intentionally refer to "parties" instead of "people" because this system not only works between two individuals, but it will also work within yourself and can even be applied to multiple people working together.

As stated before, the two parties in this system are called the **motivator**, the one doing the motivation, and the **motivatee**, the one being motivated. Motivating others starts with being able to motivate yourself. If you learn to apply this system effectively, you'll be able to motivate yourself to do anything, given enough time and resources. Although self-motivation can be difficult, there are two key advantages you'll get by starting here:

1. You get unlimited practice!
2. Once you identify and employ your own M-Props, even the toughest uphill climbs will feel like an easy cruise, and you will become nearly unstoppable.

I will teach you a series of techniques that you should use on yourself first. Once you become proficient, you can start applying them in your relationships with others.

My goal is to teach you the tools you need to motivate yourself and others so that you can create the life you want to live. It isn't going to create itself. In fact, without purposeful action,

> **You can create the life you want to live. It isn't going to create itself.**

it goes the other way. The law of entropy states that anything in nature will naturally devolve into chaos unless it is intentionally put in order. I love interfering with this law and helping people reach their full potential.

Throughout the book, I will share examples of both good motivation (i.e., ethical ways of applying positive pressure) and bad motivation (i.e., unethical applications that are more manipulative than motivational). This system is extremely powerful and can be used to create incredible results. For the comic book fans who know the line from *Spider Man* when Uncle Ben tells Peter Parker: "With great power comes great responsibility," you know what I'm talking about. Please apply these lessons ethically. By doing so, you'll find that it's not only more rewarding, it's also much easier, more beneficial, and longer lasting.

The Motivation Formula is simple and is seen in all motivational activity. This equation is the system that we know when followed properly, leads to the desired results. It looks like this:

(MOTIVATOR + MOTIVATEE) x SYSTEM = RESULT

Or

(YOU + THEM) x SYSTEM = RESULT

Or

(Y + T) x S = R

The field of psychology has done a phenomenal job of exploring and explaining how people will typically react in a variety of different situations. However, each individual person could completely contradict established norms in any given setting. Predicting general behavior is easy; knowing exactly how a person will act at any point involves a number of variables. A person's past can be filled with experiences that have molded them to act and react in different ways, depending on the situation and the stimuli.

As a husband, I'm still the same person my wife married years ago. However, the way I react in different situations can seem completely out of character to her at times—sometimes for the better, but sometimes for the worse. This is often because there's some experience in my past that has influenced how I act. Every human on earth is similar in this regard: we could even take a hundred different people who went through the same experience as children and see that each learned a different lesson from what they encountered.

Because of this, we use the Motivation Formula to motivate a person, regardless of what their background is or whether we even know their back story to begin with. Over the course of the coming chapters, we'll break down the Motivation Formula into its components to better understand each part.

This system is unconventional: to teach it effectively, the structure of the book will be unconventional as well. Each chapter will communicate a complete, self-contained lesson; you'll be able to walk away at the end of every section and immediately apply what you've learned.

I've divided the book into four parts, each of which is a separate lesson that can stand on its own:

1. **YOU**. This section focuses on your role as a motivator and how you should interact with the people you've identified as your motivatees. Knowing yourself is a critical component of being able to motivate effectively, and you might find it surprising how little most people know themselves.

2. **THEM**. Here I dial into the various aspects of motivatees, what you should assume and know going into any situation, and how to empathize with them. At its core, motivation is nothing more than finding out what someone wants deep down—even when they're not aware of it themselves.

3. **SYSTEM**. In this section we zoom out and observe the system as a whole and how the motivator and motivatee fit into the picture. I also teach what I believe is the most efficient and comprehensive system to help motivate the unmotivated. We have spent decades developing this system that we call the LP which you will hear about throughout this book and even more in depth during the later chapters.

4. **RESULTS**. Contrary to what we might think, identifying the results you're striving to achieve isn't always easy. I'll teach you how to structure motivational goals so you can predictably achieve the outcomes you want.

The ability to motivate the unmotivated effectively comes from understanding each part of the Motivation Formula and how to utilize it in unison with the other elements.

Let's break down the variables of the formula and see which part you should focus on to become a better motivator. There are three parts we can control, which are the actions we take when it comes to the Y, the T, and the S. You can't control Unmo's actions, but you can control how you interact with them. The goal of the system is to increase and multiply your R, which you can do in a variety of ways by focusing on the different variables in the equation. Don't you just love math?

If you don't truly understand who you are, what your own M-Props are, and why you feel the way you do about things, you'll end up acting like a dog who's been through surgery and is wearing a cone for the first time. He means well, but every step he takes has unintended consequences because he doesn't know how to adapt to this new reality. He runs into door jambs, knocks over lamps, and frustrates the people around him because of how clumsily he moves. If you picture your emotions and desires as the cone, and yourself as a dog, you can see how that works out in your life. Once you identify the cone, your roadblocks, and get used to its parameters, you can move skillfully.

I've developed this self-evaluation scale to give you an idea of where you stand on the various parts of the equation. As you read through the descriptions below, rate yourself on a scale from negative to positive.

This first set of questions relates to the horizontal axis: **how well you understand yourself**.

Let's find out how you're doing...

1. **Can you articulate, in one word, what one thing you need to be focusing on right now in order to have a successful week?** If you can easily identify that, the answer is *yes*; if you have to think about it to come up with a response, the answer is *no*. Be honest with yourself: there is no right or wrong answer, just your truth!

$$(no) <-----(-1)-----|-----(1)-----> (yes)$$

2. **Do you already have a list of goals that you want to accomplish this week?** If you can pull up a written list from somewhere right now or know them off the top of your head, the answer is *yes*. If it's an "off the cuff" checklist in your head or you have to think about it, the answer is *no*.

$$(no) <-----(-1)-----|-----(1)-----> (yes)$$

3. **Do you have a clear plan for what you expect to happen in your life tomorrow?** If your plan is simply to go to work and deal with things as they come up, answer *no*. If you have a written set of objectives that you're planning on achieving tomorrow, answer *yes*.

(no) <-----(-1)-----|-----(1)-----> (yes)

Net number for the horizontal axis:_____

This next set of questions relates to the vertical axis: **how well you understand the motivatee.**

4. **How would you rate your positive interactions with Unmo?** Are you motivating, encouraging, and helpful? Do you avoid sarcasm and demeaning conversation?

   The *Harvard Business Review* published an article several years ago that discussed the results of a study examining the effects of positive feedback.[2] The basic ratio they measured was the number of positive comments to the number of negative comments a team received; then the team was evaluated on how effectively they were achieving their goals. The study found that the highest-performing teams had a ratio of 5.6 to 1, meaning they received 5.6 positive remarks for every single negative remark. This is how I want you to score yourself for this section. Since you're trying to catalyze Unmo to achieve a higher level of performance, 5.6 to 1 should be your benchmark. If you're in the ballpark of this level of positive feedback, mark yourself in the positive. If you need to significantly change your interaction to reach this, mark the scale in the negative.

(needs work) <-----(-1)-----|-----(1)-----> (good to go)

---

[2] Jack Zenger and Joseph Folkman, "The Ideal Praise-to-Criticism Ratio," *Harvard Business Review*, March 15, 2013, http://hbr.org/2013/03/the-ideal-praise-to-criticism.

5. **If you had to write down Unmo's biggest goal for this week or next week, the greatest motivating factor in their life, and three things that encourage them, could you easily do so?**

$$(no) <-----(-1)-----|-----(1)-----> (yes)$$

6. **How much credibility do you have with Unmo?** If you can give them encouraging remarks and watch their behavior change in a positive direction, indicate that with a +1 on the scale below. If you find yourself constantly repeating yourself or your words seem to have little effect, circle the -1.

$$(no) <-----(-1)-----|-----(1)-----> (yes)$$

Net number for the vertical axis:_____

Your answers to these questions will indicate where you should focus most of your time. Add up the total score and determine where you fall on the following diagram. Feel free to put an X in the quadrant in which you currently fit. Again, each relationship is different. This exercise is meant to show you what part of the motivational relationship you could begin working on to quickly start seeing results.

YOU

The Beggar

You have a good grasp on who Unmo is, but you need to develop your knowledge of yourself and be a bit more consistent in your actions. Spend more time in the YOU section.

The Leader

You know yourself well and are consistent in your actions. You are treating Unmo the way he wants to be treated. As a great motivator, just sharpen your skills as you read.

THEM

-3   -2   -1

3

2

1

1   2   3

-1

-2

-3

The Loser

You are lost! You don't know yourself well, are not consistent in your actions, and don't understand Unmo well. Focus on moving out of this section. Master the YOU section before you go into the THEY section.

The Puller

You have yourself figured out and are consistent in your actions. Hypocrisy won't be an issue for you. However, you're spending little to no time focusing on them. Change the focus from You to Them.

CHAPTER 4
THE MOTIVATION CATALYSTS
The Value of a Rock Has Changed

Motivation is unique for each person and is often as varied as the DNA that makes up each individual.

As a business owner, manager, and father, it's part of my role to motivate. Like a general who moves his troops into battle, or a team captain pumping up his team for the second half of the game, a key part of leadership involves motivating others. But with everyone needing different levels and types of motivation, there is no universal solution to motivating others. There are just too many variables to be able to assume that something that worked last time would work this time—or that something that worked for one person would necessarily work for another. Granted, there are actions that can be taken once, and motivate many people, but at the core of each motivatee, there is a high likelihood that they each have a different reason why this action motivated them. Imagine if you watched the movie *Braveheart* and saw William Wallace giving his famous speech right before going into war, and because you saw it work for him, the next day you come into the office, face painted like a Scottish warrior at the end of the 13th century, and recite the talk to your team. It would wake people up, but I am not sure it would motivate your team.

People are complex and continuously changing. What they want now may be different than what they want later. I've noticed that whenever I hire someone new there is a "honeymoon phase" where little to no motivation is required: they're excited to get started, they eagerly follow instructions, and for a few weeks they're the hardest worker on the team. If I sit back and do nothing as a manager, usually within a month this honeymoon phase ends. That "whatever it takes" mentality we were both so energized by becomes a thing of the past.

It is as if the person I hired doesn't bother showing up anymore. Sure, their body is there, and the name hasn't changed, but they start acting differently than the willing and eager applicant I saw during the interview process. If I am not careful, they become a "typical" employee, unfulfilled and operating on autopilot, interested in doing only the bare minimum to get the job "done".

One of the primary reasons this happens is because during the interview stage, the typical candidate expects a simple transaction to occur. The employer offers something in exchange for the future employee's time and completed tasks. Because of how society has molded us, the future employee thinks he/she desires monetary compensation the most. So, the employee makes it clear that they are willing to do anything that the job requires them to do in order to receive that paycheck. He/she conveys dedication, eagerness, and a self-inspired drive. However, once the employee is hired and the paycheck is secured, that money goes from being something they look forward too, to something they just expect. The flaw here is assuming that money is the long-term driving factor.

Don't get me wrong, like most people, I like money. But money is just the currency that allows us to do more of what we want to do. In society, currency is of course necessary, but again, the money is not the most sustaining motivator for any human...even if we think it is.

As a business owner, I have seen how money works with people of all socioeconomic backgrounds. The best way I can describe money as a motivator is simply one word—<u>fleeting</u>. Like most individuals' spending habits, the motivation is gone as quick as the dollar is spent.

I've hired, managed, and worked beside everyone from six-figure earners to hourly entry-level employees. I've been involved with startups, as well as established corporations that are worth billions. The one similarity they all have is a pool of employees who are motivated in different ways. After working with thousands of individuals, I've discovered four "Motivation Catalysts" that strengthen the underperforming synapse that Unmo deals with and influence people to drive forward and pursue real results.

It's interesting that as universal as these catalysts are, few people can identify their own Motivation Catalysts. People are so disconnected from what motivates them, they rarely are given the opportunity to fix it. When you ask the average person what motivates them, the go-to answer is usually something like "money" or "making a difference." It often takes a hardship in life, or a massive reality check, for people to dig deep enough to learn what truly motivates them on an individual level. Authentic motivation goes very deep, and it is derived from a person's core values and purpose.

While money can be a motivator, it is often a secondary factor when you're digging deep into what drives someone. This, unfortunately, isn't well understood. Daniel Pink, a world-renowned expert on motivation

> **Authentic motivation goes very deep, and it is derived from a person's core values and purpose.**

and best-selling author, states the following in terms of motivation, "There is a mismatch between what science knows and what business does."[3] When I consult with a new company and ask about motivating factors, the first item they talk about is almost universally the compensation plan. While earning money is a foundational aspect of having a job, people can go anywhere and be paid for their time. I look at the company leadership and ask them one simple question: "Why would an employee choose to work for YOU?"

Some managers try to use a "creative comp" plan that is designed to give each employee a slice of the pie if the company does well. These plans are often described in glowing terms, like a vividly painted masterpiece filled with brilliant colors. Employees are usually disappointed when, at the end of the year, what they receive is the equivalent to a hastily drawn stick figure. A critical leadership lesson here is to make sure we're not overpromising and underdelivering when it comes to motivational assurances.

Another standard practice is to promise employees equity in the company, thinking that if they feel a sense of ownership, they'll work harder. This isn't an inherently bad idea, and in some cases, it has the potential to work as long as the company structure and direction heavily factor into the success of this motivational strategy. There are only two situations in which this approach is likely to be successful.

The first is if the mission of the company is to grow to a certain point and sell it and this mission is well known throughout the company. That gives employees something to strive toward. They are motivated by the knowledge that the more profitable they make the company, the more valuable their cut will be. If your business goal isn't to sell the company for a profit, equity stake rarely works at the individual employee level. This kind of offer is useful

---

[3] Daniel Pink, *Drive: The Surprising Truth about What Motivates Us* (New York: Riverhead Books, 2009),144.

in getting employees in the door but often fails to inspire them to produce results.

The second situation is if the company's stocks are growing at a noticeable rate and employees can see the benefit of owning equity. For decades, the promise of equity was a stable one. We knew that the economy and the stock market were stable, consistently delivering predictable growth. Over the past twenty years, however, we've seen that dynamic change. From the dot-com bubble to the housing market crash, where home equity became a liability instead of an asset, people are leery of being promised uncertain value.

Dr. Andrew Chamberlain wrote in a 2017 *Harvard Business Review* article that studies have consistently proven that what we think motivates people isn't always on target: "One of the most striking results we've found is that, across all income levels, the top predictor of workplace satisfaction is not pay. It is the culture and values of the organization, followed closely by the quality of senior leadership and career opportunities at the company. Among the six workplace factors we examined, compensation and benefits were consistently rated among the least important factors of workplace happiness."[4]

Money motivates people to come to the job, but it fails to inspire them to produce results once they're there. This has application in our personal lives as well. How many times have we "messed up" in a relationship and think, "If I just get him this, it'll fix things" or "If I buy her that, she'll feel better"? Despite all the marketing campaigns for flowers, jewelry, and designer watches, material things don't fix problems, no matter how nice they are. Solutions,

---

[4] Andrew Chamberlain, "What Matters More to Your Workforce Than Money," *Harvard Business Review*, January 17, 2017, http://hbr.org/2017/01/what-matters-more-to-your-workforce-than-money.

however, do—and the only way to create a solution is to know what that person truly desires at their core.

Our spouses, partners, and kids don't want STUFF from us. They want acceptance, appreciation, and love. "Things" can give us temporary positive feelings in those areas, but they aren't a long-term solution. Material things are only a means to attempt to fulfill deeper desires, and those deep desires are what we genuinely want.

> *Material things don't fix problems, no matter how nice they are. Solutions, however, do*

Think about what money is. Without context or a market in which to spend it, money is just meaningless paper. What it represents is the ability to do something with it for ourselves or the people we love. For some of us, money isn't even necessary to do what we really want to do; we might just need the proper environment in our workplace, home, or relationship. If you find what people genuinely want at a core level, you're equipped to motivate them.

We all want PVTT, or Personal Value Tied to Task. Finding this PVTT and shifting your focus to it will not only strengthen this synapse upon which motivation depends, but it will boost the value of the actions they take. By increasing the PVTT, you will increase the desire to take necessary action. It doesn't matter the age, experience, or background; PVTT is a universal human need for sustainable motivation. Through my time working with thousands of individuals, I've discovered four Motivation Catalysts: freedom, acknowledgment, connectivity, and support. When it comes to motivation, money, at best, is the means by which people seek to fulfill these four Motivation Catalysts.

To clarify again, money is both a reward and a tool for motivation, but not a catalyst. See, a catalyst, as a simple definition, is something that precipitates an event.

Again, people will do things for money, but it is not about the little pieces of paper they get. It is the value that they put behind those little pieces of paper that is important to them. The reason money is used in the first place is because it gives a standard for society to use to function. It allows us to understand what we are giving and what we are getting in return, but Motivation Catalysts go even deeper than the paycheck. They are why we want the paycheck in the first place.

Although a new smartphone or large gift card would certainly be appreciated by your employees, if you use Motivation Catalysts correctly you will be able to motivate others without spending much, if any, money. One of my favorite examples is of a manager who wanted to give bonuses for a job well done but didn't have the budget to do much. She created a program where she recognized people's achievements by giving them a literal rock that she had found and painted with the words "You Rock!" on the front. As simple as it sounds, this became a major motivating factor, and people proudly displayed the awards on their desks.

These were simply rocks that she would pick up from the building's landscaping before she walked in—the exact same rocks that her entire team would pass by each day. But when she grabbed a rock and wrote on it with paint, there was now an added value given to it.

What you give your team means extraordinarily little. All that truly matters is how they value what you are giving them. That feeling that they get is what drives motivation, and because of this phenomenon we will focus on Motivation Catalysts that bring the most value to each person as an individual.

These catalysts work best when they are introduced through the Motivational Path, which is the process through which an individual moves from actions to results based on internal and external motivators. Let's think about when we are working with a team member. For the sake of this book, let's assume you (the reader) is pulling most of the weight and we need to figure out how to work with our counterpart. It is felt immediately if we appreciate others or not. It is like the first impression however we can take steps to ensure appreciation is felt. Appreciation is either given by others to the individual or the individual already feels appreciated for what they do. Once the individual feels appreciated, now they understand that you are on their team. They are part of something and therefore, there is now some value behind the actions they take. At this time, although it is not necessarily sustainable, with this recognized value tied to the task, the individual experiences motivation, which causes the them to take action, and then that action leads to results.

This is just the beginning but next is how we take it to the level of being self-sustainable. It's like the small spark that starts a flame. If handled properly and given the proper elements, the small spark can become a massive sustainable source of energy. The next level is showing them more than just the value of the task but instead helping them connect Personal Value Tied to Task (PVTT)

The fastest way to bring this PVTT to individuals is to understand what it is that sparks their motivation. Which of the four

Motivation Catalysts will help not only spark the motivation but keep the fire burning even when you were not there to manage it?

There could (and probably will be) an entire book on just this concept but I want you to get a good enough understanding so that you can use them as a guide. The biggest mistake I hate seeing is when someone learns about an assessment like this and they start putting people in boxes. Let us give you a simple introduction to the 4 Motivation Catalysts (Freedom, Acknowledgement, Connectivity, and Support) along with a quick understanding of how to motivate anyone (including yourself) using these Catalysts.

1. Freedom

People who are motivated by freedom are the ones who perpetually have empty vacation and sick leave balances. They're out seeking new experiences at every opportunity. They value their time. To them, a job is usually the means to an end, and if they can see that connection to their freedom, they'll be much more motivated to excel.

Because of their desire to be out in the world, these people can seem disconnected from the rest of the team. But we need to understand what it is they desire. The biggest mistake we can make with people who thrive off freedom is trying to get them to conform to what *we* want and value. That will deflate these individuals quickly and put them on the defensive before you know it. Let these individuals be themselves, and it will seem like the results just appear. Do not just make them do things so that you can demonstrate your control over them. I promise you, that will be the fastest way to lose any influence you could have over them, and they are some of the most easy to manage individuals you will ever encounter, when treated properly

If you know someone like this, here are some tangible actions you can use to ignite this Motivation Catalyst, which help strengthen the Motivation Synapse, stimulate motivation, and improve the motivator/motivatee relationship:

- Know about what they do outside of work. It will be varied, exciting, and they will most likely enjoy talking about it.
- Recognize that time off is much more valuable to them than money or tangible objects.
- Consider a relaxed schedule or perhaps even no set schedule. If you give them a feeling of independence at work, they'll produce much better results. Allow them to have input into how they spend their time working for you.
- Create a workplace environment that focuses on individuals getting results and not just needing them to clock in just for the sake of clocking in. Find ways for them to connect what they are doing at work with the hobbies they are interested in outside of work.

If you feel **FREEDOM** is your primary catalyst, here are three things you can do to motivate yourself:

- View work as your Purpose Vehicle or in a way that allows you to see your current job to get closer to where you want to be in life. Maybe you're not at your "dream job" but if it is helping you cover living expenses so you can eventually live the lifestyle you want, then there is your PVTT. Shift your focus away from the tasks that seem meaningless to you. Instead, recognize that these tasks are a step you currently need to take to access the freedom you desire.
- Always have your next vacation scheduled and use your away time intentionally.
- Make time for you. Scheduling time for you to do the things you like will increase your effectiveness for your more mundane

tasks. Hobbies are not just a "fun idea", they are fuel for you – treat them accordingly.

What will stop momentum, build a Motivation Wall for this individual, and weaken the Motivation Synapse is:

- Not being able to see a connection between a current task and personal freedom or seeing their schedule blocking their freedom.
- Getting bogged down in administrative tasks that seem busy and meaningless
- Requiring them to attend meetings where they feel nothing is being accomplished – Meetings that could be emails
- Box-checking exercises that are monotonous and unproductive.

2. Acknowledgment

People who are motivated by acknowledgment are the ones who want to know they are doing well. They desire to be publicly acknowledged as excellent and are more inspired by a well-timed "Great job!" than they are by a bonus check or unexpected day off. This isn't because they have low self-esteem; it's simply because praise amps them up. They use this acknowledgment to create personal value tied to their actions /tasks (PVTT), strengthening the synapse between action and results.

If you know someone like this, here are some tangible actions you can use to engage this Motivation Catalyst, which help strengthen the Motivation Synapse, stimulate motivation, and improve the motivator/motivatee relationship:

- Say "thank you" or show gratitude two more times than you think you need to.
- Congratulate them verbally for hitting a goal.

- Leave an encouraging note when they have a big presentation at work.
- Remind them how capable they are, especially when they doubt themselves.
- Compliments are a must. Find something to positively recognize daily.
- Publicly praise them for a job well-done in a group setting.
- Applaud them for their positive actions first, especially if you need to scrutinize the results outcome.

Here are three things you can do to motivate yourself with **ACKNOWLEDGMENT** as your primary catalyst:

- Embrace it when someone gives you a compliment. Let yourself experience the compliment – take it in and use it as fuel.
- Take some time to focus on the positive actions you are taking toward a goal. Try creating a "victories list" where you write out two to three positive things that happened in your day. It sounds corny, but don't knock it 'til you try it. Give yourself the credit you crave.
- Be overly generous with the good things you say about and to others. The more you bad-mouth others, the more your subconscious mind feels it needs to defend itself from you. Don't become your own worst motivator- and it starts with how you speak about others!

What will stop momentum, build a Motivation Wall for this individual, and weaken the Motivational Synapse is:

- Public scolding/scrutiny/shaming.
- A lack of acknowledgment for positive actions or results
- Devaluing their attempts or actions.

3. Support

Individuals who are motivated by support are often intensely loyal. They want to know you have their back because they know that they'll have yours. If you see someone like this working late, you'll deepen your relationship tremendously by deciding to stay late and work with them.

It's important to pay attention when someone with the Support Catalyst does something for you. They often expect the same in return, even if they're not aware of it, and can get their feelings hurt if you don't deliver. They're often very fair but expect the effort they put in to be matched by others.

If you know someone like this, here are some tangible actions you can use to engage this Motivation Catalyst, which help strengthen the Motivation Synapse, stimulate motivation, and improve the motivator/motivatee relationship:

- Ask them how you can help, and then do it.
- Match their efforts.
- Take a task off their to-do list and put it on yours.
- Offer to do something that is not related to their regular work-day (e.g., get their car washed, go grocery shopping for them, pick up lunch).
- Pull your weight while you delegate. A big mistake is unnecessary delegation. Delegation is important part of management but recognize that dumping things from your plate to someone else's plate can backfire.

Here are three things you can do to motivate yourself with **SUPPORT** as your primary catalyst:

- Take time to recognize that other people are working with you. Even if you are a remote worker, others on your team are doing their job to support you.
- Let people help you. This can be hard because you are used to doing things yourself but give others the chance to help you. It makes them feel good and shows you are not alone. Speak up when you need help so others can deliver.
- Give more compliments. Although you like when others recognize the quality of work and effort you are putting out, you do not need to be told "good job." Because of this, you probably rarely do it for others. Make it a point to give one "unnecessary" compliment a day.

What will stop momentum, build a Motivation Wall for this individual, and weaken the Motivational Synapse is:

- Delegating out of laziness.
- Throwing too much on their plate.
- Hypocrisy.
- Avoidance.

4. Connectivity

If I said the word "collaborators" or used the term "team players," you would probably have specific individuals instantly come to mind. These are the people who thrive on connectivity. If there's an opportunity to plan an office potluck, they're the first ones to raise their hands. When you're in a staff meeting, they're the first people to look at someone who has been quiet and ask them for their input. If there is ever a neighborhood gathering or a family reunion, they're the ones who get the most excited!

These individuals not only want to feel connected to the work itself; they also want to feel connected to the people around them.

They are often profoundly empathetic and will be the first to notice when someone is feeling down or off.

If you know someone like this, here are some tangible actions you can use to engage this Motivation Catalyst, which help strengthen the Motivation Synapse, stimulate motivation, and improve the motivator/motivatee relationship:

- Try to get to know them as a person outside of their work.
- Value them, value the work they are doing, and value the fact that you are working together on this.
- Set aside some catch-up time either before or after the work-day, meeting, etc.—no phones allowed.
- Stop by their desk to chat about a project you're working on together. Their sense of ownership makes them like a proud parent, so a brief conversation about collaboration goes far.
- Always maintain eye contact when you're having a conversation with them.
- Remind them not only of how good their work is but also how good of a teammate they are—they take this personally, in a particularly good way.
- Send them a text to check in and see how they're doing.

Here are three things you can do to motivate yourself with **CONNECTIVITY** as your primary catalyst:

- Focus on the big picture. You are doing the small tasks for the bigger good. Give yourself a daily reminder – whether it's a visual or words, make sure you are constantly reminded.
- Be purposeful in your connections with the people with whom you need to work. Feel free to make friends with people on your team. Be intentional about getting to know new people.

- Make a goal on a weekly basis to reach out to someone and see how there are doing outside of work. Whether this is a coffee or a face-to-face conversation, be the one who create connection.

What will stop momentum, build a Motivation Wall for this individual, and weaken the Motivational Synapse is:

- Dismissing, directly or indirectly, them as a person.
- Engaging in any personal attack.
- Putting them in "time out" or any solitary confinement.

So, which one are you? We all have a mix of Motivation Catalysts that can strengthen the synapse supporting motivation, but usually there is a primary and a secondary catalyst. If you're struggling to identify yours, go to www.LifePulseInc.com/MCA to take our Motivation Catalyst Assessment. I would suggest you have your co-workers, family, and friends take it as well so that you understand exactly how to motivate those closest to you.

Once you've identified your Motivation Catalysts, you're more equipped to understand your motivatee, their own catalysts, and how to inspire them. These are the three questions you should ask:

1. What is my Motivation Catalyst?
2. What is their primary Motivation Catalyst? What is their secondary?
3. What can I do to connect the task/goal with their Motivational Catalyst (PVTT)?

Our natural tendency is to offer others what we want, but that's usually ineffective in motivating those who have a different Motivation Catalyst than us. Rewards that make all the difference for us might only trigger an "Aww, that's sweet" reaction from others—in other words, recognition of action but without any sustainable motivation behind it. Therefore, it's so essential not only to understand Motivation Catalysts objectively, but also to find out which one's matter to our motivatees. Then we can leverage those approaches in order to understand and reach them better.

Here I'd like to point out the Motivational Tree.

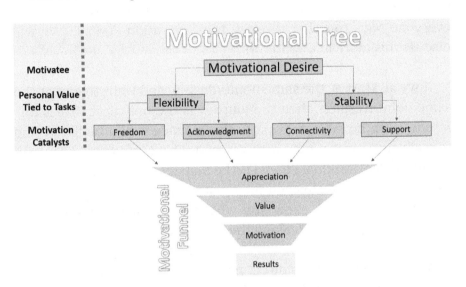

When working with one specific client, one of their biggest issues was dealing with the different generations colliding with each other. We call this the Generational Gap but by using the Motivation Catalyst properly, they were easily able to bridge this gap.

This was where we first found that people perceive value behind their actions based on flexibility or stability. This is in all areas of life but is easiest seen in the professional setting. A lot of this perception of value comes from how they were brought up. So, the older generations, in this situation were the Boomers, consistently valued things in life that brought stability for themselves and their family. The younger generations, in this case Millennials, consistently valued things in life that brought them flexibility for themselves and their family.

In order to bridge the Generational Gap, we need to start from everyone has a Motivational Desire. Expand our understanding to recognize what is their PVTT and then what Motivation Catalyst will ignite that individual. Once we have that, we start bringing everyone back together through the Motivation Funnel. (We will discuss this more in Chapter 9)

If we all start at the same point (desire), and want to end at the same point (results), then the journey is the only part that is different, With no system or path, this journey would be like trying to walk across a country with no map. This Motivational Tree on top of the Motivational Funnel is the Map for you to follow in order to effectively motivate even the most unmotivated individual. The rest of the book will show you what to do along this journey to make it easier each step along the way.

Motivation can have a direct path, as seen above, but it can also start from a point of desire at the top of the Motivational Funnel and then branch out from there. Each motivatee has a motivational desire, which generally fits into one of two main categories: stability and flexibility. Stability is for those who are looking to have all they need in life and lead a more predictable life. Flexibility is for those individuals who are usually a bit more risk tolerant if they see the payoff at the end.

The four Motivation Catalysts stem from these two desires. For the desire of *stability*, you will find the Support and Connectivity catalysts are most effective. For the desire of *flexibility*, you will see the Acknowledgment and Freedom catalysts work best.

Some people might realize that they would like both flexibility and stability in their life, but we all lean a bit heavier toward one of these desires. Be true to who you are and what motivates you. I have a lot of friends who say they would love to be an entrepreneur, and I know as well as they do that deep down, they would not want to deal with the unknown and terrifying lack of stability that is in my life. Regardless of which catalyst is most important to someone, it is merely a means to an end—a way to make someone feel appreciated and valued, which leads to motivation, which ends in results.

Motivating others is hard enough by itself; when both parties have no idea how to reach the other person, it becomes nearly impossible. The average person thinks they know what they want, but in reality, they likely have no clue. Remove this unknown variable. Discover what moves you first. Then set to know what moves those around you. This flow is fundamental to making this motivational system sustainable.

CHAPTER 5
MOTIVATIONAL PACKAGES
It's Like It's My Birthday Every Day!

Not everyone likes the same carrot.

Engagement is a crucial concept when you're working with people, and it's something we at Life Pulse emphasize with all of our clients. No matter if you are working with people in the workplace, your community, or even in your own household, engagement is necessary for there to be positive interaction and growth throughout a team. The following statistics are what drove the creation of our programs to help transform individuals and teams:

- **36 percent** – The average employee who works an eight-hour day is only productive for 2 hours and 53 minutes.[5]
- **$7 trillion** – The economic consequence of disengaged employees is approximately $7 trillion in lost productivity globally.[6]
- 450-550 Billion – The cost each year to US based organizations due to disengaged employees[7]

---

[5] Melanie Curtin, "In an 8-Hour Day, the Average Worker Is Productive for This Many Hours," *Inc.com*, July 21, 2016, http://www.inc.com/melanie-curtin/in-an-8-hour-day-the-average-worker-is-productive-for-this-many-hours.html.
[6] Gallup, "State of the Global Workplace," *Gallup.com*, 2017, http://www.gallup.com/workplace/238079/state-global-workplace-2017.aspx?.
[7] "DNA of Engagement: How Organizations Create and Sustain Highly Engaged Teams." *The Conference Board.* https://www.conference-board.org/topics/dna-of-engagement

- **14 percent** – The percentage of employees who know their company's goals, strategy, and direction.[8]
- **85 percent** – Workers across the world who are not engaged with their work.[9]
- **230 percent** – Organizations with highly engaged employees had an average three-year revenue growth 2.3 times greater than companies whose employees were only engaged at an average level.[10]
- **87 percent** – Highly engaged employees are 87 percent less likely to leave their company.[11]
- **33 percent** – The amount of people who leave their job due to boredom.[12]
- **$4,129 & 42 days** – The average cost to replace an employee and the average length it takes to backfill that position.[13]
- 21 percent – The increase in profitability due to employee engagement[14]
- **$2,400** – Increasing employee engagement investments by 10 percent can increase profits by $2,400 per employee per year.[15]

---

[8] David Witt, "Only 14% of Employees Understand Their Company's Strategy and Direction," *Blanchard LeaderChat*, May 21, 2012, http://leaderchat.org/2012/05/21/only-14-of-employees-understand-their-companys-strategy-and-direction/.

[9] Gallup, "With the Right Partner, You Can Create an Exceptional Workplace," *Gallup.com*, http://www.gallup.com/workplace/.

[10] "Executive Development," UNC *Kenan-Flagler Business School*, http://www.kenan-flagler.unc.edu/executive-development/.

[11] Corporate Leadership Council, "Driving Performance and Retention through Employee Engagement," St. Cloud State, 2014, http://www.stcloudstate.edu/humanresources/_files/documents/supv-brown-bag/employee-engagement.pdf.

[12] "Breaking Boredom: Job seekers jumping ship for new challenges in 2018, according to Korn Ferry survey." *Korn Ferry*. https://www.kornferry.com/about-us/press/breaking-boredom-job-seekers-jumping-ship-for-new-challenges-in-2018-according-to-korn-ferry-survey

[13] https://www.shrm.org/about-shrm/press-room/press-releases/pages/human-capital-benchmarking-report.aspx

[14] https://www.gallup.com/workplace/236927/employee-engagement-drives-growth.aspx

[15] Elizabeth Dukes, "Want a More Productive Workforce? Invest in These 3 Things," *Inc.com*, July 27, 2016, http://www.inc.com/elizabeth-dukes/want-a-more-productive-workforce-invest-in-these-3-things.html.

- **70 percent** – Managers account for 70 percent of the variance in employee engagement and productivity.[16]

These statistics paint a disillusioning picture of work life in the modern world. As we've moved into a post-industrial society, everything is governed by metrics. We see the value of assembly lines, automated processes, and standardized approaches. Unfortunately, we've taken that lesson and applied it to how we manage our human "resources," and we can see how well that's working.

People aren't machines. They aren't universally motivated by the same set of factors. Even studies, such as those previously cited in this book, demonstrate that the best salary and compensation packages often present conflicting data, underscoring the unique nature of humanity. Different factors influence each person's engagement even if what they say they want, is not actually what they want. When I am working with clients one-on-one, they all start by saying they want to make more money but as we break down what that means, it is much more about what they can do with that money. For one person, they might think it is a higher salary and it might be a higher salary, while for another it might be quality of life outside of work. A third person might be motivated by ownership in a project, while a fourth might not care as much about her salary as she does about a benefits package.

As a leader, it's your job to know your people well enough to find what each person genuinely wants and structure their work to maximize engagement and motivation.

---

[16] Randall Beck and Jim Harter, "Managers Account for 70% of Variance in Employee Engagement," *Business Journal*, April 21, 2015, *Gallup.com*, http://news. gallup.com/businessjournal/182792/managers-account-variance-employee-engagement.aspx.

It always amazes me how much time I see business leaders spend on crafting detailed and intricate ways to motivate their team when they've spent virtually no time asking the team what they want. This is in large part a result of how we've been conditioned to think about leadership. Management and parenting books tell us the same thing: present an idea excitedly, and your team will buy into it.

That approach works for little kids (sometimes), but its utility rapidly fades after that. If there isn't an underlying motivational factor at play that makes someone *want* to do something, the results won't be there.

Instead of compensation packages, we need to focus on creating "Motivational Packages." We need to sit down with an employee and find out what they want. Then we can structure their compensation, benefits, and work environment around making that happen.

However, another problem we face in today's often disengaged society is that people don't know what they want. You could ask several employees whether they wanted a ping pong table for the office, and they might respond with "sure." "Sure" is not a sign of motivation.

At the beginning of the book, I talked about the five Motivation Catalysts. These are the things that most people actually want in life. Each person generally has one primary and one secondary catalyst.

"Sure" is not a sign of motivation.

Motivation Catalyst	Desire
Support	Knowing I'm pulling my weight and can count on you to do the same.
Acknowledgment	Receiving verbal recognition for what I do.
Connectivity	Being part of something impactful and bigger than myself.
Freedom	Experiencing independence to live the life I want to live.

If you're trying to motivate your employees, the first thing you need to do is have them take the Motivation Catalysts test (www. LifePulseInc.com/MCA). This will give you an excellent idea of who you're motivating. The next step is to come up with a range of options that you can offer your team and align them with the Motivation Catalysts listed above that bests fits them.

Remember, the goal of a motivator isn't just to offer rewards. The ideal outcome is for the motivatees to willingly work to produce results simply because they want to. Let's use the example of a toddler who needs to clean up his room. Depending on the Motivation Catalyst that appeals to him, here are what some options could look like:

Motivation Catalyst	Question for Toddler
Support	Do you want me to help you clean the room?
Acknowledgment	Thank you for being such a good boy. Can you please clean up the room? (Follow with "Good job!")
Connectivity	Will you help me clean the room?
Freedom	Let's finish cleaning the room first, and then you can (insert whatever they like to do).

That might seem elementary, but I hope you see the principle in action. Remember, toddler or adult, humans are humans. These catalysts feed into human nature, and human nature overrides any demographic into which Unmo might fall.

Here's another example, but set in the context of an employee working on a big project with a tight deadline:

Motivation Catalyst	Question for Employee
Support	Do you want me to help you complete this project?
Acknowledgment	Our team could really benefit from your expertise on this matter. Can you please help finish this project?
Connectivity	We can celebrate as a team after we complete this project. Can we count on you to contribute and be a part of this project?
Freedom	Let's finish this project first, and then you can (insert whatever they like to do).

When structuring your Motivational Packages, you will want input from others on your team. Creating offers that help spark that Motivation Catalyst will encourage even the most unmotivated individual to become motivated.

Motivation Catalyst	Objective of the Reward
Support	Showing that they are not alone and there is a backup for their efforts.
Acknowledgment	Showing they are recognized and will be recognized for the work they do.
Connectivity	Showing that the work they do makes them part of something bigger than them.
Freedom	Showing that the work they do leads to the lifestyle they desire.

Figuring out which Motivation Catalysts your motivatees need is a huge step toward helping them develop self-motivation. Structure rewards around how they think and feel, and then give them several options from which to choose. You might be surprised how much they change and how much easier it is to motivate them when you have, and *use*, this knowledge.

CHAPTER 6
THE FULFILLMENT PHYSICAL
Checking Your Vitals

Motivation without balance rarely leads to fulfillment.

As you saw from my personal story in the previous chapter, prior to the dramatic downbeat in my life pulse, I was living a seemingly motivated life. I had a financially successful business, and I was blowing my professional goals out of the water. Unfortunately, I was living out of balance in the other areas of my life. I wasn't balanced at all. Imbalance happens when you lean on just one part of your life to hold you up while neglecting the other parts. It creates a false sense of stability. I assumed that since the business felt sturdy, everything else in my life must be too. But I never checked those other three legs to be sure.

When you visit a doctor for a physical, there are four primary indicators that they check first:

- Heart Rate
- Body Temperature
- Respiratory Rate (Breathing Rate)
- Blood Pressure

These four numbers will allow the doctor to see how well balanced your body is. If all four measures are in line with the expected ranges, it's likely that everything inside is good to go as well. If one or more of the numbers are off, however, there is usually something off balance and that's when the doctor starts digging to find out what's going on under the surface. Like these four vital signs of life, the Four Vital Signs of Fulfillment (listed below) need to be balanced through constantly checking and effectively managing your optimal fulfillment. It is something that will always need to be tweaked as life goes on. Balance through constant adjustments leads to a fulfilled life.

As I discussed in Chapter 2, from March to May of 2014, my Four Vital Signs of Fulfillment were completely out of manageable range; I just didn't know it. I realized that although there were external events impacting my life, I was the common denominator. In a terrifying realization, it was as if I was the last to recognize this. When I brought it up to others, a common answer was, "hmm, I could see that." People felt bad for me, but few were surprised. I thought I was doing well externally, but it turns out I was only fooling myself. Once I realized how far out of balance my life had become, I became determined never to allow it to happen again.

We founded our company, Life Pulse, Inc., around the concept of "bringing intentionality back to life" for all our clients. To do this, we've created our own four "Vital Signs of Fulfillment" (internal, professional, relational, and physical) to help monitor the fulfillment in our life.

Keep in mind, a "fulfilled life" will mean different things to different people, but the desire to live a fulfilled life is universal. Just like there are different body shapes and types of athletes (imagine a powerlifter trying to do gymnastics), the manifestation of a fulfilled life is as varied as the people on the planet. There are, however, key indicators—or as we call them, "vital signs"—that can be universally assessed.

Professional – The Measurement of How You Are Growing Your Career

The professional vital sign had become the primary, and almost exclusive, metric in my life in the months and years leading up to 2014. My mindset was "if business is good, then life is good." I even remember specifically thinking that I would focus on making as much money as I could early on and then focus on building a family later. Looking back, I'm grateful for the series of roadblocks I hit, because they stopped me from what could have been a massive mistake, missing out on years of valuable time with my family.

I was certainly motivated in this area, but this was solely where all my motivation was housed. It didn't translate into any other area of my life. I wasn't driven to seek growth elsewhere; I concentrated all my attention on the professional.

Physical – The Measurement of How You Are Growing Your Body

If you asked me during my time of imbalance, I would have immediately told you that being healthy was a priority in my life. Unfortunately, my words didn't match my actions. Sure, I had a gym membership and went occasionally, but I spent more time responding to e-mails and texts at the gym than I did working out.

When I did work out, I didn't have a goal. I didn't put any effort into planning a routine because I wasn't building toward anything. I was mindlessly checking a box, and as you can guess, that got me nowhere. There was no growth.

When my doctor told me that I didn't have perfect health, I dismissed it at first. I was up at 4:00 A.M. every day and working until around 8:00 or 9:00 P.M. No rest, no breaks, just work. I remember thinking that I couldn't maintain this pace if I wasn't healthy. What I didn't realize was that my stress levels were so high that my body was in constant "fight or flight" mode. My resting levels of stress were like some people's stress levels when they spike.

Years later, a medical professional showed me my cortisol levels and explained why they were so high. My body had been conditioned to handle such a high level of stress for such long periods of time that I still struggled with elevated cortisol. Just because I could deal with it didn't mean it was healthy. Physically, I looked fine on the outside. On the inside, however, my body was in constant overdrive. I never allowed it to rest. Just like a car can start but only go so far before running out of fuel, our bodies can do the same. I was literally pushing myself toward an early death.

Relational – The Measurement of How You Are Growing Your Connections with Others

This part of my life was nonexistent. For years, I poured myself into my business to such a degree that the only human interaction I had was with employees or customers. Even those relationships weren't ones I took pleasure in. I valued them for what I was getting out of the deal, but I didn't find any emotional enjoyment like you should see in a typical friendship.

I was a consumer of relationships: I gave what was needed to get what I wanted. That's no way to form relationships. People who knew me during this time might call me "a jerk" or "cold-hearted." I justified it to myself by saying that I treated everyone in the same way, so at least I was being fair. Fairness, however, isn't how humans value connection. We want a genuine experience with another person. I was so focused on work that the relational realities I created there bled over into my personal life. I certainly wasn't growing relationships in a healthy way.

I treated my relationship with my friends, family, and even my ex-fiancée like this. They were business relationships. I had an expectation that every action I took should be met or exceeded by the other person. This worked for my business partners because it was very transactional, but that doesn't work in personal relationships.

During this three-month period, I went on a retreat to try to help me connect with my own spirituality. To be completely honest, my primary motivation in attending was to network with the person who was putting it on—he was the owner of one of the largest mutual funds in the world. When I got there, however, I was told that it was a silent retreat. I love to talk, so this was a shocker. When I realized the implications (no networking!), I was initially frustrated but decided to make the best of it.

This was a critical turning point in my life and where I found myself spiritually. I was drawn to a verse in the Bible that said: "true worshippers will worship the Father in spirit and in truth" (John 4:23). This was a massive wake-up call for me. Every relationship I had was cold and calculated. I met people strategically, logically working out how it could benefit me in the long run. If a relationship ever got to the point where it didn't make logical sense, I would end it. The spiritual part of that verse really stuck out to me as the emotional side of a relationship, and a healthy connection between two people should have a balance of both the logical and emotional, or truth and spirit.

I came home from the retreat excited to share this discovery with my fiancée at the time. She pointed out that this is what had been missing from our relationship, handed me the ring, and that was it.

Life can feel safer when we don't get invested relationally, but it's also empty. It took over a decade for me to realize that there is a difference between being transparent and being vulnerable. I have never had a problem being transparent, but it is not difficult to be transparent when there is no vulnerability involved. I am a very transparent person, as you can see throughout this book. I never have a problem telling people what is going on in my life, but just because I can talk about "me" does not mean I am being vulnerable. I know I am being vulnerable the few times I can break through—when I am not only sharing the "what" but also the feelings and emotions behind it.

Now some of you are reading this, and I can almost hear you thinking, "There is no time for that weakness." Emotions do not make you weak; it is the lack of emotions that makes the relationships in your life weak. I am not saying you are to break down into tears every time you talk, but I am suggesting that you become vulnerable with the relationships that you have. So, for those of you who think they are vulnerable but in reality, are just transparent like me, here is a simple way to open.

When you are sharing your stories with those whom you care about or anyone with whom you want to build a relationship, listen to what you are sharing. If you are just being transparent, you are sharing a lot of the "what." It is like you are just reporting the news and explaining the sequence of events. To correct this, be vulnerable by focusing on the results of the "what"—not just what happened in the story but what transpired internally for you because of that happening. Why does this story matter to you, and how did it impact you? It is an easier way to answer the question few people like to hear: "How does that make you feel?"

If you think doing this makes you weak, you are speaking from a lack of experience with vulnerability. It is not easy, and you absolutely cannot be weak to do this. The weakness comes by avoiding it or letting it drag you down. Understand again, there is nothing weak about being vulnerable, and the strength that will come to you and your relationships will show you that if you have the guts to try it. Allowing yourself to be vulnerable and genuinely connecting with people is the key to relational health.

Internal - The Measurement of How Well You Are Growing Your Mind/Soul/Spirit

During my downward spiral, I realized that I wasn't putting anything positive into my life. I wasn't reading like I used to. I wasn't connected spiritually. I wasn't listening to positive music. My music selections were all geared toward what would get me pumped up, not what would feed my mind, soul, and spirit.

I remember a friend and mentor, who was the US Memory Champion, telling me that the brain remembers everything, even if we can't recall it. What I was listening to and watching had a profound impact on me. I looked at my social media interactions with fresh eyes and realized what a waste they were. I enjoyed the images and videos because they were funny or featured attractive women, but these created unhealthy expectations in my life that only led to internal decay, not growth.

I realized that the goal of life is not finding balance in the way most people think about balance. Balance, when using a scale, is about comparing two things and seeing if they are an even weight. This is why balance always feels impossible. Unlike a fixed weight on one item balanced with another, life is always changing and can fluctuate between the ups and downs in a moment. Because life is constantly changing, we need to change our perception of what constitutes a well-balanced life.

A balanced life does not necessarily mean that I am giving equal attention to all four of the vital signs. In actuality, we are on a constant journey, making sure we are at peace with ourselves in these four areas every step of the way. Am I giving the attention I deserve to each of these areas based on the life I want to live? This may seem like a difficult question to answer because it does not have a definitive, quantitative number attached to it. Instead, it can be answered only in your head and in your heart. I knew the answer, but the problem is, I never took the time to reflect on it. I focused on the one vital sign that was "producing the highest yield," and because of that, I lost sight of the other three, on which I still depended for vitality in life.

So, I now make sure that I am at peace with where I am in each of these four vital signs, each dependent on my own unique life needs. Again, the goal here is not ensuring equal time is spent on each area but that proper attention is given to each. Only you can decide what that attention entails, as every person has different metrics that indicate health for them.

The definition of "trajectory" is "the path that a moving object follows through space as a function of time."[17] If we take off from a solid launching point and follow a continuous path, we can determine exactly where we'll end up.

Let's say we go for a walk on a path but adjust our trajectory by just a single degree. After moving forward one foot, we wouldn't notice much of a difference—we'd be off of a straight line only by a

[17] Noam Shoval, "Trajectories: Analysis," *Wiley Online Library*, March 6, 2017, https://doi.org/10.1002/9781118786352.wbieg0611.

fraction of an inch. As we continue to walk, however, the farther we move forward, the more off-course our trajectory becomes. After 100 yards, we'd be off by about five feet. After a mile, we'd be nearly 100 feet away from where we intended to go.

We're talking about life, though, which has greater repercussions. So, let's take air travel as an example. If we flew across the United States from the West Coast to the East Coast and were off-course by an inch at takeoff, we'd be over 100 miles off-course by the time we reached our destination. That's just a five-hour trip. Imagine if we were taking a journey as long as our life: How far off would we be when we hit what we thought was our "destination"? It's easy now to see how people wake up one day full of regret, wondering how they got to a destination they don't like the look of.

All the choices you made got you to where you are today. We hear this all the time. So, think for a moment about where you were just five years ago and what it was you wanted. In the moment, we are usually greatly confident in our own future. As humans, even with how much the world beats us up, we tend to edge on the side of optimism when it comes to our outlook on life. If I were to ask you to paint a picture back then of what your life would be like right now without managing these Four Vital Signs of Fulfillment, the picture today may be different than what you expected back then.

As you look back on the path you took to get from where you were to where you are, it becomes clear that many choices have been made along the way—some good, some bad; some you could have avoided and some that seemed like a good idea at the time. We cannot control the outcome of our life without first looking at the choices we make throughout our life. The best way to create the future we want is to make the correct choices right now to be at peace with the actions taken in these Four Vital Signs. There will be bad things that happen all throughout life, and without peace it is often impossible for people to make it through those times. When you are at peace, and the Four Vital Signs are properly managed, it is much easier to make it through the ups and downs that life throws your way. Being at peace with the actions taken in the Four Vital Signs of Fulfillment allows us to make accurate choices that move us forward on the proper trajectory.

Let's say you sat down for one of our all-day seminars, and I offered you the choice of one of these four stools:

Which would you choose? Having one solid leg is better than nothing; at least you could lean on it for a bit, take the weight off your legs, and get some rest. However, one wrong move and everything would topple over. A chair with two legs offers slightly more support, and you're balanced on one axis, but the slightest hiccup will still knock you over.

Three legs give you your first taste of real stability, but you're still vulnerable to a variety of forces. Once you have four legs, however, you almost have to knock yourself over intentionally because the chair is too stable.

Ever since I realized the crucial nature of balance, I have started dedicating time to actively manage each of these four vital signs every week. I've also found that the priority order plays a role. During my time of imbalance, I put professional goals and needs first, and everything else fell haphazardly after that. While the priority of each of these four vital signs will vary based on what's going on in your life at any given moment, you can't neglect any one area for long without endangering your stability.

Being aware of the different 4 Vital Signs of Fulfillment helps you track changes and adapt to them. For example, if I'm on the road for a week due to business, my time with family and workout routines might suffer. When I get home, I give these a higher priority for the next week to restore balance—which ultimately leads to creating fulfillment overall.

Think of balance as the foundation beneath your feet when you're preparing to make a jump across a ravine. Like this jump, we want as strong of a foundation any time we are wanting to motivate someone. If your foundation is not balanced, you'll never make it. Your personal balance is crucial to everything else we'll discuss in the book.

When you're told to make some area of your life (for me, it was professional) less of a priority so that you can focus on the others, the natural temptation is to think that you'll be less productive. That might feel true in the short term, but one of the things you'll discover in living a balanced and fulfilled life is that each "stool leg" reinforces the others, making you better and more efficient across the board. This, ultimately, allows you to experience your desired outcomes in all areas of your life.

I often see the tendency, especially in people focused on success, to attend exclusively to the "make it" stage of life. In other words, you justify the sacrifices you're making now because you'll finally start living the life you want when you "make it," whether that's a certain income level, job title, or age. What I teach all my clients is that you need to look at your life now and determine what kind of life you want to live so that you can start on that path today.

Years ago, I was on a Granados family vacation. My brother Tony and I were having a conversation on the beach, and he asked me if I planned on marrying Maria. I answered that I was, and he responded by questioning what I was waiting for. I gave him a few reasons that made sense in my mind, but as I said them out loud, they seemed flimsy.

Tony looked me in the eye and said: "Let's pretend we're at the end of your life. You're on your deathbed. What would you give to spend one more day with her?"

"Anything!"

He kept going: "What about one more week? A month? A year?" I understood his point. I would do anything for more time with her, but for some reason I was waiting. I knew I wanted to marry her, that she was perfect for me, and that I didn't want to spend another day of my life without her, but I was still waiting. I realized that the reason I was doing this was that I wasn't thinking in the present about the life I wanted to live in the future. Each day I was waiting to act, I was adding an inch to the trajectory of the plane taking off from the West Coast to the East Coast. I was about to miss the opportunity to create one of the most powerful legs in my four-legged stool. It was in that moment that I said to myself, "There are actions I need to take right now in order to live the life I want in the future."

Start managing your life now so that you can correct those one-degree deviations before you get too far off-course. I challenge you to check yourself regularly. Our company, Life Pulse, Inc., created the LP planning system to do just this. The 9 parts of this system allows you to accurately reflect on what you have done, see what should be done, and then do what needs to be done. If you are not familiar with the LP system, you will see it later in the book If you are using our LP system, you are very familiar with how this works. When you're planning your week, set at least one goal in each of the four vital signs. When you review your week, do what I call a "Pulse Check." Basically, rate yourself on a ten-point scale and see how "at peace" you were in each area. If you are not where you want to be in any of the four vital signs, refine what you are doing, course correct, and then continue living your life.

If you embrace this concept, I can guarantee with almost complete certainty that you will live a life with fewer regrets and more fulfillment. When done properly, balance is your strength and reward. Live your life now in such a way to ensure the life you want to live later.

CHAPTER 7
THE EXCUSE OF ADD
The Choice of Joy

Focus is a choice, not a condition, and it's one we make daily.

When I was in school, I was given every label you could think of. I had a lot of trouble paying attention so the first label I received was a diagnosis of Attention-Deficit Disorder or ADD. I had a lot of energy as I grew up, so that label transformed into Attention-Deficit/Hyperactivity Disorder, or ADHD. In an attempt to help, most of my teachers basically gave me a "get out of jail free card" throughout grade school. These labels became an excuse that both my teachers and I used to answer for poor grades. As the years went on, we just added a new letter with a new disability to explain my actions, but we never corrected them. It appeared to be a good solution at the time, and I was fine with it.

These labels stuck with me throughout grade school and into high school. One day when I was a senior, I was talking with another member of my football team who also had been diagnosed with ADD and other learning disorders. He was an excellent athlete but a terrible student. Due to his diagnosis, he was able to get out of many school responsibilities while still focusing on sports. I asked him how he could have so much trouble paying attention when that season he was breaking state records that have yet to be broken. He explained that on the football field, everything moved in slow motion for him. He could see the plays develop much more quickly than anyone else, which allowed him to adapt for the opponent's next move. He was able to pay attention to multiple things at once and make split-second decisions.

This meant that he had an incredible ability to pay attention. Given the right context, he was even better than everyone around him! Although ADD is a legitimate disorder, many of the people who assume they have it merely struggle with paying attention in a particular context. My dad used to tell me that I had the energy of a grenade: if I could just take that energy and aim it like a rifle, the results would be incredible. Put me in an opera house, and you will see signs of my "ADD." Ask me about business or self-growth, and I can focus like a laser for days. Similarly, ask a student what the answer is to a math test, and they might not be able to give you the correct answer. Ask that same student a statistic for a sporting event, or a question about a video game or whatever they may be interested in, and they can discuss it with incredible accuracy for long periods of time.

We all struggle with focusing on things that don't naturally hold our attention. One of the reasons for this is that we don't see the value in the things that don't interest us. Once I learned how to control my focus, life became much easier. I could accomplish anything if given enough time and the right resources. Success, like focus, is a choice we make—not a condition that holds us hostage.

> **Success, like focus, is a choice we make— not a condition that holds us hostage.**

We need to be able to make a conscious choice to focus. Without focus, we can have no intentionality. Without intentionality, the Motivation Synapse is almost guaranteed to deteriorate, making it harder and harder for Unmo - could be you or them - to become motivated. It is freeing when you come to the conclusion that you do not have to like something in order to focus on it. In reality, it is actually quite the opposite. If we can learn how to focus on something, it becomes much easier to enjoy it.

We all have something that captivates our attention and allows us to focus with unyielding attention. These are usually the things we enjoy. Once you decide to apply that focus to things you know are important but don't naturally hold your attention, you become unstoppable.

So how do we pay attention to something that is not engaging us? I have found that the simplest and easiest first step is to make the decision to focus. Think about being in a classroom or at a seminar. There are two roles in these settings. There is the teacher/speaker and the student/attendee. With two different roles, there must be two different responsibilities. The question is, who's responsible to make sure something is learned?

The way most people see it, it is the students' job to sit there and absorb the information, and it's the teacher's job to present the information. Those are the tasks, but who is actually responsible for ensuring that learning occurs? When we are the teacher, it seems like we expect the audience to take on the responsibility to learn, but when we are the student we expect the teacher to present it in a way that is engaging and easy for us to understand. This is the opposite of how we should be thinking. We need to change from expecting the other role to be responsible for learning to taking on the responsibility ourselves.

As a teacher, it is easy to pay attention and be active in the conversation because we are usually the one leading the conversation. But as a student, how do we overcome the seemingly impossible feat of staying focused during something we feel is boring or does not pertain to us? The worst thing we can do is allow ourselves to be distracted. Usually this is done when we pull out our phone and start checking social media or our e-mail. At that point, you are so disconnected it becomes increasingly difficult to get your focus back. By taking on the responsibility to learn and enjoy, we are taking control of the situation we are in.

When we really need to focus, we are usually in one of the following two situations: learning something or experiencing something.

Learning Something

When attending an event where you need to learn something and it is difficult to focus, it can be because the teacher is terrible, the content is boring, the seats are uncomfortable, etc. The slightest thing that can distract you *will* distract you, so you need to bring your focus to the content being presented. I say to my audience, "You are going to be sitting here throughout the presentation, so I would suggest absorbing all you can; then later you can decide if you want to use it."

Instead of writing something off as boring or useless, take out a piece of paper and a pencil (or your phone if it is on airplane mode so the world doesn't beep in and bother you), and start taking notes on what is being said. The more boring or "useless" the information seems to be, the more I force myself to write. If the teacher/ speaker is not going to be engaging, I am going to do all I can to stay engaged. When they hit unprecedented levels of boring, I need to step up my game, and so I literally write down everything they are saying. It can be quite comical because sometimes I can feel the presenter giving me special attention for it, when in reality I am just trying with all my power not to get distracted.

Here is the big takeaway: no matter how bad the teacher or speaker is, no matter how elementary I feel the topics might be, since I have started forcing myself to write down what is being said, I have never felt like my time was ever wasted by someone else.

Experiencing Something

In 2006, Vince Vaughn and Jennifer Aniston were in a movie together called *The Break-Up*. It is one of Maria and my favorite movies to watch together, and we always suggest it to other couples, because it does an amazing job of depicting both sides of a dysfunctional relationship. As the breakup is playing out, they both can't stand doing what the other wants. Aniston hates going to a college football game, and Vaughn would rather drop dead than go to the ballet. So how can we stay focused during something like this—something in which we have no interest, no understanding, and no care to spend our time doing?

I found that throughout life, these situations come up no matter how much we feel we are in control. When I am doing something that I do not necessarily want to do, I spend as much time and energy as needed to find something to appreciate about what is happening. When it comes to a Broadway show, I am not as excited about the music or lyrics as Maria is, but I am excited to watch people who have spent a lifetime crafting a profession out of acting. Again, if I can appreciate something, I can allow myself to have the pleasure of experiencing what is happening. I have found that the more I take responsibility for my experience and try to understand it, the more enjoyable it is. Why choose to be miserable when you can choose to enjoy?

Imagine you are at a ballet where all the dancers are off-beat and kind of just moving around with no sync or order. Or imagine if you go to a musical where all the singers are off-key, forgetting their lines, or just running off with stage fright. Imagine if you went to a sporting event where the players were just running in circles, not following the rules of the game, even to the point of so much chaos that the players are scoring on their own team. I think we all could think of how difficult it would be for us to sit through this.

Let's put some context behind this sloppy ballet, off-key musical, and chaotic sporting event. As parents, we support our kids at events even when we wouldn't consider their performance "good." Think, for example, of the first ballet rehearsal, the first musical, or even the first football game. All three of these are described above, but when it is our kids, it is enjoyable. When I watch this, I appreciate it not because of the quality of what I am watching but because I *choose* to appreciate it.

Granted, as parents we have an unconditional love for our kids, so we can make it through some of these painstaking events instinctively. But they are enjoyable because we have attached value to them. Kids aside, this is what I found to be the easiest and simplest way to positively experience any event I attend.

Intentionally practice applying your ability to focus in situations where you would naturally be distracted. Choose an activity that would disinterest you, set a timer for twenty minutes, and practice holding your focus. Do this daily.

If we can control our focus, motivation will not be an issue. Controlling our focus is the easiest way to strengthen the Motivation Synapse in our own lives. You will be amazed at how much more you learn and how many things in life you can enjoy. Have you ever met someone who always seems to enjoy everything they do? You can do the same, and even be a bit less annoying if you'd like. When you are at an event or performing a task that you might consider boring or pointless, understand that it is *your* responsibility to enjoy what it is you are a part of. Your choice, your life, your time spent!

CHAPTER 8
MANIPULATION VS ENLIGHTENMENT
One Lasts Forever

Manipulation drives people apart, but enlightenment brings them together.

When bolstering the Motivation Synapse for our self and others, there are ethical and unethical ways of doing it that we need to be aware of. At first glance, you might think these things are subjective, but they are not. There is no gray area of right and wrong when it comes to this topic. If you are having to explain yourself, then it was probably unethical. This does not mean that the motivatee must always agree with what you did for it to be ethical, but when you break motivation down into either manipulation or enlightenment you will see there is a very clear answer as to what we are doing as motivators. Again, there is *no* gray area here.

If you're in sales, there's no insult that will hit home harder than when you are told that you sound like you're selling something. Even if they are complimenting you on how good of a salesperson you are...you never want to hear it. It's strange but undeniable. You're in sales, and therefore you should be selling, but if you're really a good salesperson the customer will disregard this fact very quickly. When you hear this feedback, it is not because the person to whom you are selling is necessarily bothered by your selling something but rather that they are bothered by *how* you are doing it. They're just like you and me; they see through the smoke and mirrors too. They immediately get the sense that you are trying to get one over on them, thereby profiting off their loss, and so their guard goes up.

I enjoy this area of persuasion (a.k.a. sales), and if you are like me, this motivational tactic can be greatly beneficial in life. However, it also runs the risk of generating negativity if you're not careful. You might have (or know someone else who has) been told at some point, "You're just trying to manipulate the situation." If that's you, this is probably the most crucial chapter in the book. For me, this is something I continuously need to work on in my life. If you're already naturally gifted at persuasion and you use this gift to manipulate other people, it will end poorly for them—and although you might not see it at the time, it will likely end poorly for you as well.

The most notorious example I can think of is the evil manipulation of Adolf Hitler and his rise to power in the 1930s. He was able to use incredibly effective and profoundly manipulative motivating techniques to enhance the synapse of a large group of people. These people were scared and desperate to take any support that came their way, not realizing the unimaginable could happen. Today, it seems obvious how morally and ethically wrong this was; at the time, though, many people were convinced that Hitler and the Nazi Party spoke the truth. Germany was so defeated after the First World War that all they were motivated to do was to survive.

This seems hard to believe for many people. Why would anyone follow someone as grotesquely evil as Hitler, let alone allow him to do what he did to Europe and its people? This is where some serious manipulation came into play, and history explains the context behind this climb to power. Germany was struggling financially after World War I. In 1921, Germany was given a bill for over £6.5 billion to help offset damages caused during the war. After poorly managing this debt, the German mark was basically worthless by

1923. This mismanagement of money caused hyperinflation to completely debilitate the German economy.

To put it into perspective, in 1918 a loaf of bread would cost £1. Within five years, the same loaf of bread after hyperinflation ended up costing £200,000,000,000 marks. When bread is that expensive, the country is in a bad place.

Already hurting domestically, Germany received financial help from America, but then, as you may already know, the US stock market had crashed in 1929, devastating America. As they were the economic leader of the world at that time, many other countries felt this pain as well. Germany, already an economic disaster, was just hurt even more so. After this blow to their economy, the German unemployment rate rose to over 30 percent. They needed help. And with this desperation, one starts to feel like they need to look for something new—anything from anyone. At this point, most people were beyond unmotivated; they were hopeless and were willing to grab onto anything that could help shine some light on their current situation.

Hitler did what many immoral leaders in history have done: he helped the people get back on their feet, and then the moment things started getting better for the common person, he took advantage of the trust he had established. He was able to convince most German citizens of his beliefs regarding why the downturn had happened in the first place. And better yet, he knew what needed to happen so that they would never have to experience these economic conditions again.

In modern-day America, it may be difficult to understand how anyone could think that way. However, if we take a closer look, we can see that although more extreme, this situation is not an isolated one.

No matter when you are reading this book, you could easily look at the current political climate and find people using these exact same techniques today. Politicians are trained to create a false sense of security by taking credit for an issue that has been fixed, then pointing fingers at other people, naming them as the reason for the problem all along.

So, let's get to it. It is vital to understand manipulation in order to beat it, and to strengthen the Motivation Synapse there are two primary ways we can motivate people:

Fear (using force to coerce the motivatee)

or

Love (using understanding to compel the motivatee)

Fear can be incredibly effective in the short-term. History has proven that. It will build a connection between action and outcome to strengthen that synapse, causing people to act fast. But this rush to act will always be short-lived. Not only is the effect short-term, but fear must be continuously applied and steadily increased for the motivation to stay with the motivatee.

One example would be a mugging: a bad guy comes up, puts a gun to your head, and tells you to empty your pockets. Few people would voluntarily empty their pockets and give everything they have to a stranger, but we all act differently when affected by fear. Now, you might be shaken up for a while and feel quite violated, but the motivation to keep giving your possessions ends the moment the gun is no longer pointed at your head. Once the thief stops forcing you to give up your possessions, you stop.

An alternate situation would involve you walking down the same street and encountering the same outcome, but in this scenario, let's connect the synapse using a different motivational proposition (M Prop) This time, the person who stops you is asking for donations for a cause that means something to you. The person who is asking might not even know what drives you to do so, but he watches in wonder as you open your wallet and give everything that you have to a stranger. You might even chase him down to give him money. When you are connecting with that individual through a sense of love and understanding, you'll be happy that you gave him money long after the experience is over.

That's the fundamental difference between manipulation and enlightenment. Manipulation, whether seen or unseen, drives people apart. Enlightenment brings them together. As good people wanting to better the society in which we live, it is our obligation to enlighten as many people as possible. That's why I wrote this book.

I genuinely believe that if your mouth is moving, you're selling something. Whether you're a doctor attempting to convince a patient how to live a healthier life or a parent trying to shape a child's behavior by explaining the consequences of their actions, you're seeking to motivate them to act differently.

As humans, we're prone to selfishness, and this is something we should always remain aware of as we navigate our communication with others. We tend to advocate for what we want, and there's nothing inherently wrong with that. The difference between manipulation and enlightenment, however, is how it affects the other person. If they end up on the losing end, then we have most likely manipulated them. If they end up benefiting, we've enlightened them.

Sometimes it isn't clear-cut. One person may feel like they are trying to enlighten the other, while the person on the other side feels like they are being manipulated. These are very real perceptions that people may have that shouldn't just be brushed over. Your goal, as someone who is better equipped after reading this book, should be to do your best to find a way to create a win-win out of any situation.

The best motivators can find the win for the motivatee faster than the motivatee can on their own. If you sit down with an honest and ethical salesperson, if you decide to purchase you will walk away happy, feeling better about yourself. The reason is simple: the salesperson took the time to figure out what a win for you would really look like; then they made it happen. Because of this, you were willing to part with some money in return.

Be conscious in your communication. You want to make sure that you're not just focusing on getting what you want, especially if it comes at a cost to another person. Earnestly seek win-win scenarios; if there isn't a win for them, there often isn't a long-term win for you either. Bridging this gap and strengthening the Motivation Synapse is enough to overcome these roadblocks, but we want the synapse to continue to perform well on its own. Think of it like this: when you cut your arm and it starts bleeding, you could grab a towel and apply pressure to make it stop. However, the second you stop applying pressure, what happens? It bleeds. Yes, it will work, but you are constantly having to apply pressure. Wouldn't it be better just to get a couple stitches, let the body naturally do what it does, so that you no longer need to use force?

Of course, there are always going to be times when not everyone wins. There will also be tough decisions that need to be made and processes that need to be followed. What I am asking of you is simply to take time to see if there is any possible way for a win-win to happen. Focus on motivating in the right way for the right reasons. Take time to hear what the other person needs and seek enlightenment instead of manipulation.

CHAPTER 9
ARISTOTLE, FRIENDS, AND A RAT
Motivation Through the Years

Science can predict the outcome but doesn't correct the problem.

Science has helped us predict human behavior in a general sense, but when it comes to motivating someone, there are too many variables to predict how someone will act with absolute certainty.

I'm a huge fan of personality tests and other similar assessments. They can be especially useful for helping us better understand ourselves and those around us. The biggest mistake I see people make when introduced to the findings, though, is when they seem to forget that this is only an assessment of the subject, not a definitive answer to who the subject is as a person. Because of that, most people use these tools to put themselves, or others, into a behavior box. "Because the test said that he's an (insert acronym, number, or whatever cute animal they were assigned), that means he'll react in this way." Don't fall prey to using these assessments to excuse someone's actions, because at some point, the subject could, and most likely will, act differently than his quiz result that stated his personality is like "Chandler from *Friends*."

Although personality tests are interesting indicators, they are not definitive guides. As a result, even knowing someone's personality indicators will leave you occasionally surprised by their actions. Please do not forget what Daniel Pink said from an earlier chapter—essentially, that science is telling us one thing, but business is doing the other.[18]

The subject of motivation has been an ongoing topic of discussion for millennia. Although many scientists and philosophers have studied this through the years, we have yet to arrive at a perfect understanding of what truly drives people to make decisions. The closest we have come to a universal philosophy of motivation is when it became clear that tangible things seem NOT to motivate people as much as intangible things. Long story short, we can't put people into boxes and just assume they will live there. To be an effective motivator, we need to observe, ask questions, and listen to those around us to start to be able to understand what truly motivates them.

In the fourth century B.C., Aristotle introduced the Seven Causes in his book *Rhetoric*: "Thus every action must be due to one or the other of seven causes: chance, nature, compulsion, habit, reasoning, anger, or appetite."[19] At the time, this was a radical proposition.

Nearly 2,400 years later, in 1890, a Russian scientist named Ivan Pavlov was doing a study to understand the digestive system of mammals. What he didn't realize was that he would discover a bedrock principle of psychology in the process.

He observed that when the dogs were presented with food, they salivated. Over the course of the study, he noticed that the dogs began salivating whenever they saw someone wearing a white lab coat because they had started to associate the appearance of someone wearing that outfit with food. This even happened when the person wearing the jacket didn't have any food with them.

---

[18] Pink, *Drive*, 144.

[19] Aristotle, *Rhetoric*, trans. W. Rhys Roberts (Mineola, NY: Dover, 2004), 38.

Pavlov started to ring a bell whenever it was time to feed the dogs. Within a short period of time, the dogs would begin salivating at the mere sound, even when no food was brought. The Russian scientist coined the term "classical conditioning" to explain this behavior. He found that when a neutral stimulus (in this case, the bell) was associated with an unconditional stimulus (the food), the subject will eventually be conditioned to respond in the same way in the presence of the neutral stimulus as he did with the unconditioned stimulus.

In the 1920s, a fellow named John B. Watson decided to see if this principle could be carried over to humans. In his experiment, which certainly wouldn't pass ethics criteria today, he took a baby called "Little Albert" and gave him certain things that he enjoyed, such as a monkey, a dog, a rabbit, and a white rat. Personally, it would have been my last pick, but Albert liked the rat most of all, so Watson used this as the core of his experiment.

Every time Albert would reach for the rat, Watson would bang two pieces of metal together, making a loud noise that would scare the baby. Over time, he conditioned fear responses in Albert that were triggered every time he saw the rat. Eventually, the fear response became so intense that Albert wouldn't accept anything from Watson because he associated everything he received from the scientist with fear.

This is a concept known as "generalization," and what we have referred in previous chapters as Motivational Walls. It is something you'll encounter with most of the people you try to motivate, whether it be in the positive or negative sense. Watson demonstrated that phobias were often conditioned responses, and we've found that many people who are unmotivated or difficult to motivate have experienced circumstances that have conditioned them to feel a certain way about a particular situation. Most likely, this experience had nothing at all to do with you.

Let's jump forward about twenty years. In the 1940s, Abraham Maslow wrote a paper called "A Theory of Human Motivation," which stated that our behaviors are driven by our needs and our needs are pursued hierarchically. In this paper, he introduced a pyramid that has come to be known as "Maslow's Hierarchy of Needs." The graphic shows how humans have specific needs but seek to satisfy needs at a given level only once all the ones beneath that level have been met.

The foundation of the pyramid is comprised of physiological needs. When basic necessities like breathing, food, water, and sleep aren't met, the last thing on your mind is which MBA program you should apply to. When we're focused on survival, we have no desire even to think about higher-order needs.

As our needs at each level are satisfied, we begin to shift our focus to the next levels of the pyramid and seek satisfaction in those areas instead. Self-actualization, which we describe as personal fulfillment or when a person knows "why they are here," is the capstone of the image. But we can experience true fulfillment only once the first four levels have been met.

Each of these studies and principles shows that there is cause and effect when it comes to motivation. That is where this Motivation Synapse exists. There is no effect because there is no cause. Unmo is not able to connect the action and the outcome.

So, motivation continues to be studied, but the findings show that although motivation works in a particular way, what motivates others and ourselves is constantly changing. What might motivate a motivatee one day, may not motivate them the next. Our external environment and experiences are massively influential to our motivation levels. And to be effective more times than not as motivators, we need to recognize that the only constant in motivating others is that they will not be constant. Thus, we will have to continuously adjust our actions based on their needs and change with them.

All these studies point to one central concept: there are quite a few ways we can force someone to act a certain way in a given situation. Although many of these findings were

> **The only constant in motivating others is that they will not be constant.**

negative in nature, the principle they illustrate is that someone's behavior can fundamentally change given the right stimuli. Remember, all science can do is predict outcomes (sometimes), but predictions cannot influence the outcome. This is where we, the motivators, come in. We are the ones who can correct behavior simply by strengthening the Motivation Synapse.

When approaching a situation where you're attempting to motivate someone, the first lesson you should recall is Aristotle's Seven Causes. Think about what might cause this person to act the way they are. Once you understand this, you can remember Maslow's Hierarchy and identify where their unmet needs likely fall. Unmotivated people have unmet needs, and they can't progress to higher levels of human satisfaction until those needs are met.

This is where positive classical conditioning and generalization come into play. In situations where your motivatee struggles, you can begin to introduce positive reinforcement and encouragement to act differently. Stay persistent, and over time you can change someone's associations with certain situations from negative to positive.

The flip side of this should give us a sense of caution, however. If we can create positive associations with someone, we can do the same with negative connotations. Being very intentional about the effects that you want to have and are having is crucial.

Although these scientific principles can help you better understand and predict human behavior, there is no perfect, universal solution. The bottom line is that you have to seek to genuinely understand someone's behavior and underlying triggers to motivate them effectively. Knowing their Motivation Proposition and using their Motivation Catalyst will allow you to strengthen the weak synapse that is hindering their motivation.

Think about someone you've been trying to motivate and reflect on the reasons why they may struggle. Work through Aristotle's Seven Causes, Maslow's Hierarchy, and think about the conditioning and generalization they might have experienced. Consider how you could use positive conditioning to reverse these effects, find their M-Prop, use their Motivation Catalyst, and motivate them. Start from basic needs and move to life desires. Get to the bottom of what it is they really want. This is how we will find the road map showing us how to help motivate the unmotivated. From this point forward, run through this exercise in your mind whenever you encounter someone who is difficult to motivate.

CHAPTER 10
MODERN-DAY MOTIVATION
Get Woke

In order to motivate, we need to understand and articulate the purpose behind each task.

Before the 1960s, authority was something you weren't supposed to question. During the 60s, American culture shifted: now questioning authority is more common than blindly accepting it. Neither approach is better than the other, although both have their advantages and disadvantages. Some leaders deserve their position of authority and are confident in the role they are in, while others fear the day someone will ask them a question they can't answer.

One of the noticeable changes in a power dynamic is a subordinate's willingness to question the "why" behind the task. Of course, this situation is highly contextual and isn't necessarily good or bad. However, put simply: if someone is asking the question with the intention of gaining a deeper understanding of the task, that's positive. Conversely, if someone is essentially challenging the authority's right to assign that task, it is negative. In either of these situations, a leader (or motivator) should always be able to justify the reason for the task. If you always have a reason for asking someone else to do something, you'll gain their trust. However, if you don't have a good reason, you'll quickly lose credibility.

From the beginning of time, humans have all been inherently motivated. Some have a better ability to understand why there is value in the task at hand while others need to be given the reason to them as if a meal served on a silver platter. Either way, modern understanding of motivation is showing us that the modern-day motivation is drastically different than what we have been doing for generations prior. In 1963, a group of scientists, Leeper, Greene, and Nisbett examined the difference between intrinsic and extrinsic motivation and rewards. Motivation, in these studies, consisted of the things that the motivatee was seeking. Things like autonomy, belonging, curiosity, and meaning made up the list of intrinsic motivators. When the motivatee successfully pursued intrinsic motivators, what he received were intrinsic rewards, which were things like fulfillment, purpose, value, and experience. These are things that can only be experienced internally and that stay with the individual long after the task or job is complete.

Extrinsic motivators, however, are things that the motivatee could receive from others. In the classic example of the stick and the carrot, the carrot is an extrinsic motivator because it's a tangible item that one person can give to another. When we are operating on the basis of extrinsic motivation, the motivatee and motivator can both see the outcome of the motivation and reward. Extrinsic rewards often decrease in value soon after they are received.

In 2011, Adam Grant and Justen Berg from the Wharton School at the University of Pennsylvania identified a third type of motivation and reward. They termed their discovery "prosocial" and called it a massive missing piece in group settings. Prosocial motivation gives us the desire to protect and promote the well-being of others; it is an inherently altruistic behavior inherent in all of us. Humans like to help others because the act of helping gives us a sense of value and worth. The two gentlemen wrote:

> *Prosocial motivation more strongly predicts persistence, performance, and productivity when it is intrinsic*

rather than extrinsic; citizenship behaviors when it is accompanied by impression management motivation; and performance when manager trustworthiness is high. Prosocial motivation strengthens the relationship between intrinsic motivation and creativity, core self-evaluations and performance, and proactive behaviors and performance evaluations.[20]

There's a saying that "there's no way to do an unselfish deed." The premise behind the proverb is that when you do anything at all for someone else, you're receiving something in return. I think this is true, even if what you receive is just the good feeling of knowing you helped someone by holding a door open.

None of these motivational factors are inherently "better" than any of the others, but they do work differently. If you're seeking mechanical skills and simple tasks that can be performed on a repetitive basis, extrinsic rewards tend to work well. The motivatee thinks: "If I do this, then I get that." It's a very straightforward set of expectations with a clear line between task and reward.

If you're attempting to foster creative behavior, however, intrinsic rewards are likely to be more effective. When you solve a problem, a puzzle, or a riddle, you get an internal feeling of satisfaction. That's far more likely to be a motivational factor than a piece of cake.

When we combine these in an environment that encourages prosocial behavior, we can develop team members who are self-motivated. This is what motivation looks like in the 21st century. Instead of picking one that you think will do better, you can use all three.

---

[20] A. M. Grant and J. M. Berg, "Prosocial Motivation," in *Oxford Library of Psychology: The Oxford Handbook of Positive Organizational Scholarship*, eds. K. S. Cameron and G. M. Spreitzer (Oxford, UK: Oxford University Press, 2012), 28–44, http://psycnet.apa.org/record/2011-19765-003.

Rewards at the end are still great to offer, so there is your extrinsic motivator. Then tie in a way to ensure some of the feelings of the intrinsic motivators while making it clear to the motivatee that what we are doing is benefiting others more than ourselves and more than just me, the motivator.

Giving a reward at the end of a task is at best a temporary fix, as the truly unmotivated still could have a sluggish Motivational Synapse that is keeping action and outcome disconnected. When it comes to a creative or ongoing project or task that needs to be completed, each second, they work without reward, that synapse gets weaker and weaker. By adding the intrinsic reward and prosocial reward, you are making this task larger than them. You are bringing value to the tasks that they might not have seen before. You are making the task bigger than the action. Unmo is now part of something bigger than themselves. It is not about finding which one works; it is about finding a path from the idea to the result that will tap into all three of these motivating factors. Trust me, you will see results faster and with less effort than you ever have in the past!

Be a 21st-century motivator. Help your motivatee find their intrinsic motivators and allow them to express prosocial behaviors. Equip them with the tools they need to complete their assigned tasks, and always be ready to explain the reason why you need them to do something. Then, at the end, when they reach the result, make sure there is a final reward as icing on the cake!

KNOWING YOU

We tend to think that everyone else is the problem, but we never really spend time getting to know ourselves—our strengths and weaknesses, our positive and negative traits. Our natural tendency is to believe that if we could only fix everyone else, all of our problems would disappear.

There is *no room* for hypocrisy in motivating others. The first part of the Motivation Formula is the most important: YOU. If you had to spend the rest of your life focusing on one aspect of the formula, you'd get the most benefit just focusing on yourself. First start by completing the Motivation Catalyst Assessment (www. LifePulseInc.com/MCA) we discussed prior for yourself before having you as your team to do it.

As we transition into the THEM section, remember that none of these techniques will work until you have the YOU solidly established. Hypocrisy is the number one reason we fail to motivate others. If a failed business owner tries to teach me about money (unless they're telling me about all the mistakes they made), it's going to be difficult to see validation in what they say. If someone living an unhealthy lifestyle tries to give me tips on how to live a healthier life, I probably won't get excited about their tricks of the trade.

However, when someone who is a self-made multimillionaire wants to tell me the secrets to financial success, I'm all ears. If a professional athlete gives me tips on improving my physical performance, I'll listen all day long.

As humans, we naturally crave authenticity. When you apply these motivational factors in your life, people's likelihood of listening will grow exponentially.

In this section, I do not care if you feel you are the most motivated individual on the planet, you'll need to hear this. I mean, if you're that motivated, it shouldn't be a problem, right?

The content in the YOU section of the book examines what the individual needs to do for themselves. We all need to make sure we are in a good place to motivate others. That means, we can always work on ourselves. This part of the motivation formula is talking about the YOU or the one doing the motivating. As you get used to using these for yourself, you will be able to suggest these to Unmo or other individuals to help build that internal, self-sustaining motivation. As you, the supportive motivator, can share from your experiences of using these techniques in your life.

The Motivation Synapse can fail in anyone and at the most unexpected times. Remember, "motivated" is not a character trait; it is a current state of mind. You may feel motivated now, but there will be times when you're not. You may not need the techniques in this chapter right now, but I can tell you, from one human to another, at some point this section may save your life. Read it now so you have it in your head for whenever you may need it.

You are also going to want to understand all these principles so that you can help Unmo implement them in his/her life. Giving Unmo this book will only work if he/she is motivated to read it.

CHAPTER 11
DISSONANCE IS DISTURBING
How to Avoid Hypocrites & Being One

You can never know what is best for yourself and others unless you know yourself and others.

Hypocrisy is heard while it is spoken, but wisdom is heard long after. You can't tell other people how to live their best lives if you're not doing it yourself. Have you ever received fitness advice from someone who is out of shape or investment advice from someone who was bankrupt?

Sometimes, the people we love most are the worst at this. They tell us that they know what's best for us but can't seem to apply those lessons in their own lives. Someone who motivates out of fear is a hypocrite; they're too afraid to live the lessons themselves. Conversely, people whose driving force is love and understanding will tell you only what they've already tried and proven themselves.

You can't motivate someone until you understand them, and since motivation starts with you, you must know yourself first and foremost. It might seem challenging to motivate another person, but if you can't even motivate yourself it will be impossible to share that with others. They'll only ever see you as a hypocrite.

If you want others to be honest, you need to be honest. If you want others to work hard, you need to work hard. If you aren't doing what you want your motivatee to do, why would they do it?

Give them a reason to value what you are saying, give them proof it works! As the old cliché goes, actions speak much louder than words.

Two statements help me put this in perspective better than anything else:

"I've been wrong, so others are allowed to be too."
"There is no true winner of an argument."

It's difficult to truly live by these principles 100 percent of the time, but that's where the first statement comes into play. Give grace to yourself and others. If I start to get angry at someone else for being wrong, I remind myself of the times when I've made mistakes. I've found that makes it virtually impossible to get upset.

The second statement reminds me of the difference between an argument and a discussion. The goal of an argument is to win, making the other person a loser. The goal of a discussion is to understand, seeking to make both of you winners.

Out of all the lessons I describe in this book, these two are the hardest for me to apply in my own life consistently. Knowing myself, however, means I know my weaknesses, and although I do not spend a ton of time worrying about my weaknesses, it would be foolish not to be aware of them.

CHAPTER 12
ARE YOUR BUCKETS FULL?
Empty Buckets Are Full of Wasted Space

Balancing your buckets makes it easier to walk.

During my "Heartbeat" in 2014, I was completely empty. Internally, relationally, professionally, and physically, my whole life was in shambles. I needed to refocus myself. I needed to better myself. At the time, I really didn't know what I needed besides needing something to change—and fast.

I started working on myself and found that with all that I had lost up to that point, I needed to start building my life back to the level I wanted. I needed to rebuild my self-value. You commonly hear about how important self-confidence and self-esteem are, but self-value is something I rarely, if ever, hear about. Is there a difference? I believe there is.

Self-confidence has to do with our internal faith in our ability to do something. Self-esteem is how I feel about myself. Self-value, on the other hand, is what I think I deserve in life. In times like my "Heartbeat," it is easy to feel that I do not deserve anything. In fact, when tracing it back, this downturn started when I stopped caring about my self-value. It was the first thing that got taken away, and ironically it was the first thing I needed to build back up.

At this point in my life, I felt like I had little to no value to offer myself or others, and because of that there was no need to be motivated. When we value our self, motivation becomes natural. As our self-value is lowered, motivation seems increasingly pointless. So how can we make ourselves (others) value ourselves (themselves)?

Through this rebuild, I discovered that by attending to three measurements of self-value that we call Value Buckets, I was able to maximize my self-value. These three measurements are how we value our self, how we are valued by others, and then finally the value we bring to others. As I was pulling myself out of this low point in my life, I realized that I needed to keep these three Value Buckets full and balanced. What I found was the more I would fill these buckets, the more motivated I would naturally become.

People tend to live up to their own expectations of themselves. These expectations tend to be correlated with the fullness of each Value Bucket. As the level in the buckets are lowered, so are our self-expectations. The way I describe these three Value Buckets are:

- Value Bucket 1 – Me for Me – This is the bucket I need **me** to fill **for me**.
- Value Bucket 2 – Others for Me – This is the bucket I need **others** to fill **for me**.
- Value Bucket 3 – Me for Others – This is the bucket I need **me** to fill **for others**.

It is important to remember that for our life to be fulfilled and our self-value to be maximized, we need to make sure all three Value Buckets are constantly getting filled and refilled. But filling up three buckets separately is no easy task, and at some of life's low points it is nearly impossible. However, I quickly realized that I did not have to do it all myself. I am responsible for Value Buckets 1 and

3, where I am the one filling them. I just needed to start with those buckets and then allow others to fill Value Bucket 2.

At my low point in life, all my buckets were empty, but the second I started filling them it was like they filled up easily and constantly. The more they were filled, the more they could hold and, low and behold, the more my self-value increased. It was like a perpetual cycle of growth that allowed me to get back on track faster than I ever thought possible.

Value Bucket 1 – Me for Me – Pouring into Self

What I was putting in front of my eyes, channeling into my ears, and imprinting on my mind was pure junk at that point. Sure, there were positive inputs from books and speakers I would be exposed to, but the problem was that negative inputs tended to imprint stronger in my mind. I could listen to multiple feel-good books and then go down the rabbit hole for just about five minutes, immediately offsetting the hours of positivity that I had just built up. Negative inputs tend to stick more tenaciously than the positive.

Part of the standard safety briefing before any flight is an explanation of what to do if the oxygen masks are needed. Parents are always told to put their own masks on before they help their children. When Maria and I fly with our kids, I always wonder if the masks were to drop, if I would put my mask on before my kids'. The smart thing to do would be to follow instructions, but sometimes we tend to forget about ourselves for the sake of others. While putting our mask on first may sound selfish, the reason why it is important is simple: if you collapse from lack of oxygen, you won't be able to help your child. You must make sure you're taking care of yourself enough to be able to help others.

Motivating others works the same way. You can't truly motivate others unless you are taking care of yourself. That doesn't mean you need to be perfect to motivate others, but you need to be filling this bucket regularly to help make motivation easier for both parties involved. The first step for me was working on my inputs: what I heard, what I saw, and what I thought. I found that it took only three adjustments to ensure better inputs. I changed what I listened to—from music that I gave no thought to what I was hearing and just focusing on how energized it would get me to things that were positive in nature like self-growth, audiobooks, podcasts, and motivational talks.

I also realized that even with the positive inputs in my life, I was negating them by putting pure filth before my eyes. It was nothing that society wouldn't consider "guys just being guys" or "normal," but it ran the spectrum from pornography and violence in videos to who I followed on social media. I decided that I needed to consume only things that would build me up. To rebuild myself, ever since this low point I make sure that I avoid anything toxic. The simple way I do it is creating a line that I do not want to cross. What has worked best for me is reminding myself to avoid things I do not want my kids knowing I was engaged with or engaging with themselves.

This might sound extreme, but for me—especially at that time of my life—it was necessary. If this is something you do not feel you need to do, that is your decision, and please understand this is not me judging you. This is just what I needed to do. If you're in doubt, try it for a week and see how it feels.

Personally, I had to completely overhaul my auditory and visual inputs so that I could control what I was thinking. I found that when I cut out negative inputs, my thoughts were easier to manage. I discovered that when I had my headspace right, getting back into making the right decision in all parts of my life was a lot easier. Everything from my internal thoughts to my physical activity seemed more manageable than before.

Value Bucket 2 – Others for Me – Get Poured Into

Asking for help from others can be difficult when things are fine. When you feel like you're at the lowest point in your life, it becomes much harder. I want you to practice four words: "I need your help." Be humble and sincere when you say this. This isn't just asking for a hundred bucks—this is a much deeper request and will be well received by most.

There are people in your life who would drop anything to help you. If you asked, they would answer. You would do the same for them, but for some reason it's much more difficult to ask for help than it is to give it. The more you practice asking, however, the easier it becomes.

If you are not comfortable asking others for help, I would suggest two things. First, get over it. Know that people like helping people. They want to help others, and they feel valued when they have the opportunity to do it. Also, we are all broken in some way, shape, or form, so trying to come across as perfect is easily recognizable as a front. There is little to no benefit in doing that. Instead, be honest and humble, and you will see that most people are willing to help.

The second thing was a deceptively simple solution given to me by a mentor of mine: journal. Get your thoughts out of your head and onto paper. This is immensely powerful, but especially if you are not comfortable asking for help from others just yet, this can work for this bucket in the meantime.

After my mentor found out how confused I was feeling and how badly I wanted to feel better, he told me to use two different colored pens while journaling. Black was for any time I was venting and writing out my thoughts, worries, fears, questions, and frustrations. Any time I had an answer or a solution, I was supposed to use red. I do not care what you call this internal voice that answers, but I can tell you that seeing your thoughts on paper makes things a lot clearer. Call it intuition, call it the universe, but for me I call it God. I got all my thoughts out where I could see them; and once that was done, the answers came almost automatically. My mentor had been using this process for decades, and the longer he used it, the better it got. Any time he doubted what was happening in his life, he'd go back and read his journals and see how clearly things had worked out in the past once he relaxed, listened, took the right actions, and sometimes just got out of his own way.

Value Bucket 3 – Me for Others – Pouring into Others

In the fifth grade, I was full of energy but wasn't directing it positively. I wanted attention, and the way I got it was by being the student that every teacher wished they didn't have. It was the "Matt Show."

From being a loud and disruptive student to bragging about failing a test or assignment. I found ways to get attention, but it was rarely in a positive way. Because of this, I started falling behind academically at an early age. I had trouble with reading and writing, and every teacher I'd had up to that point had essentially let me talk my way out of anything. That was when I met Mrs. Pyzer. She was the first teacher who didn't put up with my acting out.

One morning, Mrs. Pyzer was frustrated that I was talking while she was reading something to the class. She suggested that since

I felt the need to talk, why didn't I just read the rest of what she was reading for us? I looked at the paper that she had in front of the class; it was a simple few sentences. It was then that she unintentionally discovered in front of the whole fifth-grade class that I could not read. After testing, it was found that I was barely at a first-grade reading level. She knew that she had to teach me to read. She also knew that I wasn't listening to anyone, so teaching me to read would take her undivided attention. Her solution was nothing anyone ever tried before, but it was genius: she made me leave her class and go to the younger classrooms to help the students get ready to leave for the day. Now, as you have heard earlier, I did not care what type of attention it was, as long as it was attention. Even something so simple as leaving my class early to do anything was a win for me. For the first time in my life (and I was too young to even realize the power of this at the time), I realized that pouring into others not only benefits them, but it also benefits the pourer. It brought more value to my own soul and brain, and I felt more fulfilled. This "bucket" of pouring into others is one of the most effective, but often most neglected, tools used to make sure we are on the right track. While you need to avoid a savior complex (you're not doing this to run from your problems), this should be a major focus area of your life.

During the "Heartbeat" stage of my life, I didn't think I had anything to offer. Several months before, however, I'd made a commitment to volunteer at a youth leadership program called Eagle University. I'd attended this program myself as a student, and to this day it is still the most impactful thing that I have ever done. I didn't want to go, but I had made a commitment, so I followed through. I was able to serve hundreds of kids by introducing them to topics that would change their lives. Ironically, it did far more for me than it did for them. This was one of the things that helped me get back on track.

There are three main parts to this process. You can start developing your Value Buckets wherever you'd like, but all three of them need to be flowing. I found that sometimes, especially when in a funk, it was easier for me to pour into others first. If I focused on pouring into others and allowing others to pour into me, my buckets naturally started to fill. If you are making sure both sides (the bucket for others and the buckets for you) are being attended to properly, it's easier and more enjoyable to accomplish internal, physical, relational, and professional goals. No matter if you are working on your own life or working to motivate others, an individual will feel maximum value when these three buckets are filled and expanded.

You can think of these buckets as something you need to carry. If you had all three buckets on a stick on your back, you could understand the importance of balancing the buckets on each side so that the weight is evenly distributed. One thing that makes these buckets so unique, is when you fill them in a balanced manner, it is as if the weight of the buckets becomes lighter and easier to carry. If you disregard the buckets, it is as if an unseen weight is constantly weighing you down. Making this walk we call life much more challenging than needed.

When balancing these buckets, it is important to understand where each bucket sits. The buckets for you would be on one side, and the buckets for others would be on the opposite side. Just like the walk with the buckets of water, when your Value Buckets are balanced, your walk through life feels more like a confident and effortless stride vs a constant and strenuous "strive" through life. Same walk, same weight, just feels lighter due to better balance. If one side is unbalanced, it is still possible to walk, but it's a lot harder.

So, here is how it works. Value Bucket 1 and 3 are for YOU and are on one side. The Value Bucket for OTHERS is on the other side.

So, it looks like this image. The right side is YOU. In these buckets, you need to pour into yourself and allow others to pour into you. The left side is for OTHERS. Now, this image shows three buckets, but know that these buckets can grow and expand as you continuously fill them. They will never overflow, but if improperly balanced they can overwhelm.

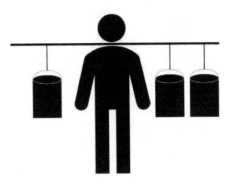

The most successful and fulfilled people are constantly filling and expanding all three Value Buckets. Your impact on each bucket does not have to be equivalent, but the three buckets need to receive the appropriate attention they deserve. To expand the buckets, self-growth is needed. The easiest way to keep this side expanding is to get yourself in a good place and then start finding as many people as you can who will help you fill your bucket in return. These can be mentors, friends, family, a boss, etc. But be careful! If you just filled your side of this equation your walk will be difficult, and the weight will feel unnecessarily heavy. Also, you're at risk of living with regrets later, wishing you did more for others or had a larger impact on society. The only way to keep true balance is by expanding the side for yourself while also expanding the Value Bucket related to the other people in your life.

This is where real fulfillment comes in, and it's where you see people start to hit levels that even they never thought they would experience. You can add as much to each bucket on either side as you want, as long as you keep them balanced. How are you going to let others pour into you? How are you going to pour into you? How are you going to pour into others? Here are ways to expand all three buckets evenly. Remember, if one side is off-balance, it is difficult to walk.

Value Bucket 1 – Pour into Self

Make sure that you are intentionally exposing yourself to positive influences. Don't forget good in = good out; bad in = bad out. Go through your social media and unfollow anyone who has a negative impact on your life. If you read something and it negatively impacts you, get it out of your sight for now. You can always bring it back later if you want, but I doubt you'll be interested once you feel the difference it makes when you intentionally bring goodness into yourself.

Review your music choices, and make sure you feel built up from listening to them, not brought down. Consider adding audiobooks or positive speeches to your playlist.

Think about what you're seeing in the movies, TV shows, books, and magazines that you're choosing. It's either positive, negative, or some kind of inert filler—and even the neutral filler isn't adding anything to your life. Choose only positive influences. These don't have to be big steps, but you do need to be seeing consistent progress.

Value Bucket 2 – Pour into Others

This can be difficult if you're in a place where you feel like you don't have anything to offer. Remember, though, you don't have to be perfect to help someone out. You just need to show up and be authentic.

When we serve others, we receive a benefit as well. The primary objective should be to add to the other person's life in a positive way, but don't ignore the rewards you get out of it. We develop an appreciation for our self-worth and a better context for how significant some problems are—and how small ours often are in comparison. You'll rarely encounter someone recently back from a service project in a Third World country complaining about problems they're facing at home. For some people, this experience is long-lasting. For others, it is just a few days until their world engulfs them again. That is why we need to be expanding these buckets constantly until it becomes our new outlook on life. We gain an incredible sense of gratitude for what we have from helping others, even if our lives are hard sometimes. The more you help others, the better and more grounded you'll feel.

Finally, some practical tips: if you're struggling with an addiction, serving other people with addictions might pull you back in. Avoid situations that can throw you off track until you are ready and find another area in which to serve. Look for churches, shelters, or local organizations with volunteer opportunities. If you can't find anything that feels like a good fit, reach out to your local magistrate, and ask for recommendations.

Value Bucket 3 – Get Poured Into

Find someone who can pour into you. This can be a mentor, family member, or even a stranger. If you feel there is no one out there who will help you, I am telling you now, that is not true. Remember, people like helping other people. This is especially true when the person they are helping is coming from a humble and honest place.

If you have had issues finding people who will pour into you, then you need to look at two things: the internal and the external.

First, the internal: Are you open to letting people pour into you? Men are known to have a MUCH harder time with this on the surface, but it is not a gender issue. Women have a difficult time with this too. Both men and women want to come across as confident and strong to others, but we need to be careful not to confuse what these concepts actually mean. People want to help people who need help. People also want to bring truth to a situation. What that means is, if you act like you do not need help, not only will people not give you help, but they will tend to let you know that you do need help. Very counterproductive.

For some reason, we as humans feel it is our responsibility to tell someone who thinks they have it all together that they don't. Then, if that person tries to show that they do have it all together when we know they don't, we make sure to make it clear to them that they do not. It is as if we are letting a blind person know they are blind. Both parties already know this truth, so why do we feel we need to push them on it?

We need to choose not to be closed off and "tough" and instead decide to be open and vulnerable, which is true strength. The best way to do this is to be honest with who you are, where you are in your journey, and what you have done. Like I said before, honestly saying to someone, "I need your help" increases your chance of getting the answers you are looking for. To dive even deeper, I would say, "Here is what I am looking to do, here is where I've been, and I have no clue how I am going to do it. Can you help me?"

Second, the external: With whom are you surrounding yourself? We need to make sure that we are around people who have what we desire and can teach us what they did to get it. In other words, do not just look at the surface; really search to see what fruit they bear. What results have they been able to get, or what experiences have they been through, that they can share with you? I found that no matter how broken or put together you are, reaching out externally works best if you are you. The good and the bad which when brought together is you, even if you don't like it. If you are presenting yourself in this humble and honest way and still not receiving anything positive in return, that is when you should start looking elsewhere.

I challenge you to take inventory and work to balance your Value Buckets every week. Make sure you're pouring into yourself and into others, as well as getting poured into. As you are working to motivate others, you need to make sure that they have all three of these buckets constantly being filled in their life. If the buckets are balanced, the next challenge is to continue to pour more into others while letting more "others" pour into you and challenge your motivatee to do the same.

This is not as hard as it may seem. To most people, this concept is foreign, but it actually comes quite naturally to humans. This does not mean that you have to spend your whole life filling all three Value Buckets each day. Sometimes you will do more for others, other times you may do more for yourself, and at some points in your life you will need to be poured into by others more than you can pour into anyone. Just make sure all three of the buckets are balanced by giving them the appropriate attention they need overtime. What balance looks like is something that you can decide, but if you feel that any one of the buckets needs no attention, I challenge you to rethink your reasoning. There is always room to pour into others, and the more you do, the more water you can carry and the more fulfilled your life will become.

CHAPTER 13
LIVING LIFE SEVEN DAYS AT A TIME
From Monday to Sunday

The best way to live your life is seven days at a time.

Life can be overwhelming, even in the best of times. When you're struggling, as I was during my "Heartbeat" phase, it can seem downright impossible. You can't see the possibilities in the future; you can see only what's right in front of you. The furthest I could think was a week out. My mindset became: "If I can just make it to this weekend, I'll be okay."

Goals were nonexistent, and that became a habit. Even after I came out of this time, I wasn't consistently setting goals. I didn't realize this until one night when Maria and I were sitting in our new house, just married, and talking about the future. The subject of physical goals came up. She looked at me and, as lovingly as she could, asked: "Do you even have physical goals?"

My immediate thought was: "Of course, I have goals. I teach goals for a living!" When I tried to express them, however, I realized that the goals I had (be healthy, stay in shape) didn't have any formal definition, start, or end point, or a plan to get me there. I immediately got on my computer and looked for the hardest thing I could do. I wanted to challenge myself.

When I came back to the conversation, I told her that I had signed up for an Ironman. Her jaw dropped. For those of you who don't know, as I was not fully aware when I made this impulsive decision, an Ironman is a triathlon comprised of a 2.5-mile swim, 112-mile bike ride, and then a full 26.2-mile marathon to top it off. I didn't have a bike, goggles, or running shoes when I signed up. Not being prepared for what I just signed up for was a small part of why I was so out of my element. I have used every and any excuse to not to workout. I understand why I need to do it, but I have never enjoyed it before, during, or after. Prior to this I might have gone to the gym a couple times a week. These few times I went, I probably spent more time walking around answering emails then actually getting a good workout. Needless to say, going from my amazing ability to avoid workouts to voluntarily doing one of the most intense training someone could get into... it makes sense why there were some doubts.

Now even though I did not like working out, as discussed in the chapter prior "Excuse of ADD", when I stopped focusing on working out and started focusing on this journey I was taking to achieve a goal, I was able to get excited about putting in the time and effort. Remember, I needed to find my own PVTT and for me I needed a bigger goal then just going for a run, bike, or swim. I trained for months with a coach and team in Atlanta until finally I was ready. As I was about to jump in the water, the reality of what I was about to attempt hit me: 144.7 miles in 17 hours or less. I looked over at a friend and said: "This is crazy. We voluntarily signed up for this?"

Moments later, we jumped in. At that point, I was committed: you either swam and kept up with the pack, or the thousands of people behind would swim right over you. My focus narrowed to a single thought: *Breath, stroke; breath, stroke; breath, stroke.* Once I found my rhythm, I realized that I had a lot of time to think.

I mentally reviewed the months of training. It had never felt real until this moment, in the water swarming with bodies that were packed so close I could feel people grab my feet with each stroke. The whole thing felt so unnatural that I just started laughing. When you're swimming, the most important thing to focus on is breathing. That's not easy to do when you're chuckling. The cycle kept repeating itself: I'd swim for a bit, then laugh at how absurd this whole thing was, then get back into a swimming rhythm, only to repeat the process a few minutes later.

When I finally saw the exit, I got excited: I'd survived the part that I was most likely to die trying. I ran up the ramp, exchanged high fives with a couple of complete strangers, then climbed onto my bike. I had trained so much that I felt amazingly comfortable with this. I fell in with a group of people who were going at the same pace, and for the next five hours, the routine became: pedal, drink, eat, repeat. The temperature was ridiculous: it was 97 degrees in Chattanooga, Tennessee, which also meant there was accompanying humidity. My time on the bike left me with a great tan, but very dehydrated. After 116 miles on the bike, it was time to dismount and start the marathon.

My first step was a disaster: my legs didn't work. They were literally stuck. After several attempts, I panicked. I looked over at a volunteer and said rather loudly, "My legs don't work!" Her advice was simple but profound: "Pick it up, then fall forward. One step at a time." I was so delirious; I took her words literally. I picked up my right leg, threw it forward, then fell onto it. I was able to hobble to the tent where I could put on my running gear.

I came out of the transition, said "Hi!" to Maria, my family, and my friends who had been following me, then started the run. A mere 400 meters in, my legs still weren't working, and I hit the first incline. I wanted to go—I *needed to go*—but my legs weren't cooperating. I looked down at my watch and realized that I had enough time to walk the whole course and still make it before the cutoff.

At that moment, one of my coaches ran up and asked how I was. I shook my head and told him that I was off-pace and couldn't get my heart rate down. He looked me dead in the eye and said: "People are dropping like flies. Take it one step at a time; just keep moving."

That was the second time in just a few minutes that someone had told me that. The problem was that 26.2 miles equals a bit more than 55,000 steps, and that number was slightly intimidating. However, as crazy as it sounds, that's exactly how I finished the race—one step at a time. I remember finding landmarks—the next turn, a stop sign, or an oddly shaped tree—and telling myself just to make it to that point.

One of the most memorable points came at the 25.2-mile mark. My coach was with me at the time and shouted: "One mile left! Want to run?" I looked at him, smiled, and took off. Let me pause for a moment and clarify that. At this point in an Ironman, "taking off" doesn't mean sprint. It merely means that I went a bit faster. That last mile, which I call "the longest mile" although it was only 0.6 percent of the race, felt so far away. I actually started counting my steps: I'd go as high as I could before I lost count, then start over.

When I finished, people kept congratulating me like I'd won a medal at the Olympics. Although this was a significant personal accomplishment for me, I thought they might be going a bit over-board with their celebrations. What I didn't realize until later was that this particular race had one of the highest DNF (Did Not Finish) rates in the course's history because of the heat.

The race taught me that sometimes, it's not about looking at the long-term reality. Sometimes, it's a 2.5-mile swim, or a light post 800 meters away, or sometimes just the next step, literally. We need to be comfortable breaking down parts of our life until they're easy to manage. For most people, that tends to be a week.

A month is too long, a day is too short, but a week is something we all can handle.

A week gives you the ability to make changes as needed. You can adjust rapidly, without getting too far off-course. Think about what you have going on over the next week. Make goals, plan out your course, then check in with yourself at the end of the week to see how you did.

Living life one week at a time makes it easier to connect actions and outcomes, which gives more value to the current actions taken. Time is something that can weaken the Motivational Synapse. You have heard the adage that "time heals all" when talking about relationships or experiences, but that doesn't work with motivation. The more time there is between actions and outcomes, the more the synapse will deteriorate. Living one week at a time gives a safe and manageable deadline for you and Unmo, while still creating some urgency to get things done.

Commit to planning your week every week. Find a system that works for you. We have developed the LP system to do just this. If you haven't yet, go to www.LifePulseInc.com/MyLP and get yourself a copy of the LP. It will guide you through this new outlook on life. Be flexible enough to adapt for the inevitable interruptions and unforeseen circumstances but hold yourself accountable to your plan. At the end of the week, review how you did, adjust as necessary, then plan for the next seven days. Every week, though, take a moment to reflect on how this seven-day period fits into the larger scheme of your life. Where are you going, and how successful are you at getting there?

CHAPTER 14
BE A. P.R.O.
Be the Celebrity You'd Like to Be

Those who don't choose to look very rarely ever see.

Surfing has been an incredibly eye-opening experience for me, and I think the experience of catching and riding a wave is analogous to life in general. The basic process for surfing involves a simple recipe, which can be summarized by being "a pro," represented as the acronym A. P.R.O.

Aware
Patient
Ready/Reflective
Open

The first step in surfing is to swim out into the ocean and wait for the right opportunity. Just like life, sometimes this happens quickly, and sometimes you have to wait for quite a while. When you're out there sitting on your board, you become acutely aware of how big and powerful the ocean is and how small you are in comparison. You become hyperaware of every sensation: the temperature, the movement of the waves, and the brush of something against your foot. If you aren't aware, you'll never seize the opportunity you know will come.

Surfing involves a lot more waiting than it does riding a wave. Not only do you have to be aware of when the opportunity is going to come, but you also have to be prepared for the possibility of waiting a long time before it eventually comes around.

While you're being patient, you can't lose focus. If you forget the importance of being aware, your mind may go numb, and then you won't be prepared for that opportunity that's just out of sight, coming toward you with the force of a monster wave. The best way to maintain readiness is to be reflective, continually thinking about what happened the last time, what you need to do better this time, and all the steps you'll take once it's your moment to shine.

Finally, you need to be open. Sometimes opportunity doesn't look exactly like you thought it would. Massive waves are small when they first appear on the horizon. You have to be sensitive to the energy building beneath the water and open to the possibility that a small, liquid ridge could be hiding the best ride of your life.

I learned to apply this process in my relationship with Maria. When we met, it was less than ideal timing. She was in a long-term relationship that was headed toward marriage, and I had just gone through a very abrupt breakup. Maria wasn't very fond of me at first, but over time we became friends, and then awfully close friends. When her relationship ended and she became single, I leaped at the opportunity. I knew this was the woman I wanted to spend the rest of my life with, to be my best friend, business partner, and the mother of my children.

We got serious very quickly, and that was the source of a lot of unsolicited opinions from our family and friends. They thought we were crazy. With both of us recently out of profoundly serious relationships, our initial foray into dating each other was called everything from a rebound to a fling. Both of us, however, knew there was something more to it. When people ask me what made it work, I tell them that it was being Aware, Patient, Ready/Reflective, and Open.

Our philosophy throughout the relationship was that we were just going to let it happen, and it happened quickly. I was always aware of what this could be. She was my equal, my counterpart, and my soulmate. I wanted her for life.

We were married quickly after the engagement, had a child, and moved into two homes all within our first year of marriage. Although this might seem counter to the definition of "patience," that word doesn't mean just waiting around. *Merriam-Webster* gives four different definitions of the word "patient":

1. Bearing pains or trials calmly or without complaint
2. Manifesting forbearance under provocation or strain
3. Not hasty or impetuous
4. Steadfast despite opposition, difficulty, or adversity[21]

One of the reasons that our relationship moved so quickly in such a positive way was because we were ready for it. We did not move before our wave came. To early or to late could have ruined the whole ride. Our previous relationships had given us an excellent sense of what we didn't want in a partner, so we were able to move past the basics rapidly. We were continually reflecting (not dwelling) on our past, applying the lessons we had learned in a way that fostered increased growth and intimacy as we moved toward marriage.

Finally, we were both open to the possibility of "forever." Neither of us were focused on casually dating and wasting time, so when we decided that we'd grown close enough, we moved into the next stage without any hesitation. We put the relationship first and didn't allow our egos or selfishness to get involved.

---

[21] "Patient," *Merriam-Webster*, http://www.merriam-webster.com/dictionary/patient.

This application is short and simple because all you need to do is be comfortable waiting for the wave and prepared for when it comes. It goes against everything we have been taught about being motivated. Normally we are told to go, go, go, but sometimes we need to wait, wait, wait. Not out of laziness or fear, but because it is just not time to move yet.

Surfing is a lot like life. You aren't in control of the waves that move you—you're only in control of how you ride them, and this makes the difference between drowning and having the time of your life. If we make wise choices, put ourselves in a position to catch the wave, and practice being A. P.R.O., the wave does all the work and we just get the thrill of riding it.

Waves can be opportunities or challenges. What makes the difference is whether you're ready for it, waiting to turn any chance into an opportunity. The process is also a learning opportunity. The best surfers sometimes don't time waves properly, get dragged under, or get whacked on the head with their own surfboards and are embarrassed in front of friends and family. Learning from your mistakes and getting back on your board to catch the next wave are what matters.

Being patient can feel like you are letting things pass you by, but in reality, you are just waiting for the right opportunity. Being intentional about your waiting is one of the hardest things to do. Now think about what this will do with the Motivation Synapse. If you wait for the right wave (opportunity), your actions are going to be causally related to the result. Remember, that is the key to curing the plague of demotivation: keep your actions and outcomes connected. If you try to surf every little wave that comes your way, you are bound to catch one eventually, but you are taking so much action to get extraordinarily little result. This is why people get discouraged. Instead, be A. P.R.O. and make sure you are putting your energy not into just any wave, but the correct wave, and you will see instant results from the actions you take.

Be A. P.R.O. in all parts of your life. Be aware of what's happening, patient for what might come, reflective as you wait, ready when it happens, and open to the possibilities that are out there.

CHAPTER 15
SELF-CONFIDENCE IS BUILT ON SELF-KNOWLEDGE
Do You Know You?

Self-confidence is impossible to have without true self-knowledge.

Long lasting self-confidence can't be taught. It can only be gained through an intense struggle of becoming aware of yourself, then accepting who you are: the good, the bad, and the ugly. When you are aware of and comfortable with that reality, you become self-confident.

Over-confident or cocky people, who are usually using a front to cover something up, can often struggle with accepting who they are. Cocky people aren't comfortable talking about their feelings or vulnerabilities because they haven't accepted those parts of themselves.

A common barrier to self-confidence is the inability to accept who you are right now. As a self-proclaimed "self-growth nerd," I can sympathize with the tendency to focus on who we will become and think we'll accept that version of ourselves when they show up. We believe that growth precedes self-confidence, but that's the opposite of reality. When you accept yourself, growth is inevitable.

Self-confidence isn't one of those things you "kind of have." You either have it, or you don't. It's like being wet: when you're wet, you're wet. Once you reach the level of self-acceptance, self-confidence can quickly follow. It is a relationship you have with yourself that is strictly a choice you make and once that choice is made, life starts to get a lot easier.

The most important part of motivating the unmotivated is working on yourself. Motivation is contagious, and people who have it naturally foster it in others. If you give an unmotivated person a task, it's hit or miss whether it will be done well, on time, or sometimes at all. If you're motivated and work side by side with someone who is unmotivated, however, no matter how unmotivated they start out, they'll likely end the project with a different mentality.

When you are physically with them, it is easy to motivate them because it is like you are the constant bridge making the connection for the synapse. However, the goal of motivating the unmotivated is to help them recognize their PVTT so the motivation continues even when you are not there with them. This is what allows self-motivation to happen no matter how unmotivated Unmo may be. Unfortunately, you can't just tell Unmo your opinion about how he/she should change. Unmotivated people seem to have a doctorate in arguing and making excuses, and you sharing your opinion is a typical catalyst for this habit to kick off. This is because they cannot connect the outcome with the action. They are just focusing on the actions.

If you looked at what I had to do in my life to get myself ready for the Ironman, you might think I am crazy—even knowing my desired outcome. Now imagine if I was doing all of that with no race at the end—just two to three workouts a day with no end goal. That is how Unmo sees these actions.

I've learned, however, that it's nearly impossible for people to argue with personal experience. If you say, "I think you should," the natural retort from Unmo is "Well, I think I shouldn't." If you start off with: "This is what worked for me, and it was incredible," then the only options they have are to ignore it, mock it or accept it. Connect your past experiences with your current way of life, and if they are positively correlated Unmo will be positively affected by your comments, even if he doesn't show it.

Remember that the first step toward motivating the unmotivated is learning to apply these lessons in your own life first. If YOU do what you want Unmo to do, it's easier to get him to tag along. As I said in the previous chapter, there's no room for hypocrisy in motivation.

CHAPTER 16
LOW MEANS LOW
Share, Don't Compare

Lowest and highest can relate, but lower and higher can only compare.

We tend to speak in terms of the lowest and highest points in our life. But when we fall prey to speaking in "lower" and "higher" terms, we are now comparing. If we want to truly relate, we need to make sure we are not focusing on whether or not our experiences were lower or higher than someone else's. Instead, we need to focus on lowest and highest and use relative experiences to connect. This will enable us to always be able to relate to those with whom we interact.

The lowest point in my life was my "Heartbeat" moment, and it's covered in Chapter 2. Since I've already told the story, if you'd like you can jump back to that chapter to review it. Bottom line: Life was tough, and it was the lowest I ever felt about life to date.

People live their life wondering why bad things happen to good people. When I hear that question, I always think about how it is impossible to answer, because it is all subjective based on everyone's definition of good and bad. The only thing that we do know is that both good and bad things happen to both good and bad people. To simplify it even more: things happen to people.

I used to hear other people's stories of something hard they accomplished. For example, people climbing Mount Everest.

Sometimes we sit there in the audience and think, *I just can't relate.* Or we hear someone telling a heart-wrenching story of a tragedy in their life—again, *how can I relate without a similar tragedy to refer to?*

The bottom line is, as soon as we have taken our first breath, we've all had our highest point in life and our lowest. As time moves on, there are more data points. Some are higher and some are lower, but they are constantly accruing with each breath we take. The details, and the context behind them, can be scattered all over the positive/negative spectrum. However, to each of us, our highest and lowest point is just that—our own individual experience. If my lowest point in my life was stubbing my toe, it is different than most others' lowest point. But because I have experienced my lowest point, I can relate to other people's lowest points.

It is all subjective and 100 percent relative to every individual. We live in a society where we feel the need to experience exactly what others experience to connect with them, but the details of the story are just ways to express what happened, not ways to make us experience the same feelings. I do not know what it is like seeing a loved one killed, and I have not personally summited Everest, but I do remember what I felt like at my lowest and highest points in my life. Because of that, I can, to a degree, relate to anyone else's story. Like them, I've lived a life and experienced both highs and lows.

We all have a point that we identify as the lowest moment in our life and comparing one another's is pointless. Pain is subjective and relative. What tears one person apart might be a matter of course for someone else. You might have had a close family member pass away when you were in your twenties, and this destroyed you. For someone who has experienced war or lived in a gang-infested area of an inner city, it might become part of normal life despite its being very traumatic. Conversely, you might have a physical disability from birth that is no longer a big deal for you—it's something you've always had. Allow someone else to lose their sight, hearing, or a limb, however, and it can feel like their life is over.

I share this for one simple reason: you can be comfortable knowing that *your* lowest point is indeed that—entirely your own—and you don't need to justify it by comparing it to someone else's pain. You could listen to my story about losing all of my money, being publicly embarrassed, and watching my relationship end unexpectedly, then just sigh and tell me that I should look on the upside; at least I still have both of my legs. If someone said that to me during my lowest point, I probably would have punched them.

Pain is intensely personal, completely subjective, and that is totally fine. When we are motivating others or our self, we need to meet the motivatee where they are, no matter where it is. There's no need to compare who's high is higher or who's low is lower. Instead, connect your high with their high, or your low with their low.

Even when I am motivating myself, I sometimes need to connect what I am trying to overcome or accomplish in the moment with things I have been through in the past. We need to know what our experiences are and what they mean to us. We need to rely on experiences rather than expectations, because experiences have past outcomes—outcomes that are known and causally related to the action. With an unknown outcome, there is little to no way for anyone to connect actions and outcome. Motivating based on expectations and comparisons is almost a sure way to let yourself down and for your motivatee never to achieve what is expected of them.

Don't feel the need to compare the details of the events in your life with others to see value and impact. Don't use comparisons to build your pain up or tear it down as this will lead you to the lonely inability to connect with the people in your life Avoid framing your situation as better or worse than someone else's situation. Instead, accept that all humans, from the beginning of their life, have experienced the highest and lowest point in their life, and that point will continue to shift as they gain more experiences. Because everyone has had a highest and a lowest point, we can relate to anyone's situation, human to human, rather than thinking we need to compare the levels of pain or happiness we have experienced. In doing this, it will allow you to connect with anyone and support them in whatever situation they are facing. If you can relate, you can connect. If you can connect, you can motivate.

If you can relate, you can connect.
If you can connect, you can motivate.

CHAPTER 17
MAYBE EINSTEIN WAS RIGHT
Predicting the Future

The best way to know where you should go and what results you should get is to look back to where you were and what results you have obtained.

Predicting the future is a tantalizing concept and one that has inspired untold numbers of books and movies. We haven't yet figured out how to do this perfectly, but we're actually better at it than you might think. We do it in nearly every area of our lives, but we just tend to call it "forecasts" or "estimates."

Arguably, the most well-known example would be weather predictions. It's not uncommon to hear jokes about meteorologists and how often they're wrong, but as soon as there's a storm, the first thing we do is tune into the Weather Channel. We do the same with road trips when we check to see how long the drive will take or with financial markets when we ask our broker for projections. It's relatively simple to get a pretty accurate estimate of the future—anything from shipping lead times to presidential election outcomes—and the way all of this is done is by recognizing the present while looking at the past.

If you learn how things have happened in the past, you can often estimate how they'll occur again in the future. People are no different: how they've acted before is a good indicator of what they'll do again. If you're curious about what motivates you (or someone else), look at what has driven you (or them) previously. Motivation is a strange thing, however, because we tend to treat it differently than every other aspect of our lives. We think things like: "If I only had a bit more money, I'd be able to do X," or "If I could just have a few more hours in the day, I'd accomplish Y." If we examine how we've utilized our time and money in the past, though, we'd see the same habits, tendencies, and errors. Until we learn from the lessons of our past and address them in how we're presently living, there's no reason for the future to be any different. The amount of money or time that you have will not fix the way you are using either. The core issue is still there. If the synapse between action and outcome is not functioning well, then doing more of what is not working will just give you more of what you do not want. There is no other long-lasting solution than strengthening this junction.

I was once asked a simple, but confounding, question by a mentor: "Why are you here?" I explained I was there to meet with him. He went on to ask me deeper, "Why are you here? Why were you put on this planet? What is your purpose?

I couldn't answer that question because it seemed so broad. He gave me a series of questions that helped structure my answer, and we've replicated that in the "Purpose" exercise I do with clients all over the world. When I went through that exercise, I realized that the answer to the future wasn't in front of me; rather, it was behind me.

My purpose became noticeably clear:

> To grow myself as wealthy and knowledgeable...
> ...to help others reach their own potential.

When I realized this, life became amazingly simple. That doesn't mean it was easy; I still faced challenges and hardships. However,

I know where to focus my time and energy. I know what the target is at all times. Any time I have a task or an opportunity, I can run it through my purpose statement and understand how it fits into my life. Once I recognized this and leveraged this in my life, I wasted less time and began to feel like I was getting somewhere. This not only empowered me, but it also enabled me to better guide and motivate others.

Most people do not know their purpose. It takes time. Motivated people might not be able to articulate their purpose in sentence form, but they know it. It could be there subconsciously but bringing it to the conscious mind makes the motivational game a whole lot easier. Those who have no clue what their purpose is will have trouble connecting it to anything.

As you try to find your purpose, or as you are helping Unmo find theirs, we have seen a consistent format for true purpose statements. It seems to break down to a simple sentence that states: I *take this action...in order to generate this outcome.* Simply put, there is a direct connection between the actions in your life and the outcomes you desire. When you look back at my purpose, you will see clearly how it fits into this format:

ACTION I TAKE	To grow myself as wealthy and knowledgeable...
TO GENERATE THIS OUTCOME	...to help others reach their own potential.

As you have heard throughout this book, this connection between action and outcome is the key to staying motivated and motivating others. When you live according to your purpose, it is nearly impossible for the Motivational Synapse to underperform.

You can use our "Purpose" exercise by reaching out to us through our website (www.LifePulseInc.com) or you can determine it on your own. The bottom line is you need to take some time to reflect on who you have been and how you have lived. What brought positive results, and what brought negative results? You can use the past not only to determine your overall direction in life, but also, on a smaller scale, to evaluate individual decisions. Think about the times in your past when you've faced a similar situation and how you handled it. Was the outcome what you wanted, or could it have been improved?

It may seem strange for you to review your own past. I mean, it is your past, you already lived it. Just because you lived it doesn't mean you recognized the value of each event. Being in the present allows you to better understand this value from your past. It is like when you see the ending of a movie which then explains all of the clues given throughout the movie to tie everything together. A good movie gives you a moment of revelation at the end.

The clues of the life you are supposed to live in the future are sprinkled throughout your past. Now that you are able to see the story as a whole, you can start finding trends. These trends will help you predict how you will act or react in the future. Also, it will show you what will bring fulfilment to your life and what will be draining to your life.

Once you do this, I would suggest having Unmo do it as well. This will give you both a great understanding of how to connect your tasks to your purpose, enabling actions and outcomes to become more interconnected. When an individual knows and uses their purpose statement, even if they are the most unmotivated person you know, it will give them a chance to self-motivate. If you, the motivator, know what their purpose is, it allows you to help them each step of the way.

Review your past to determine where you should be going in the future. Do this with any individual decision. If it's a small decision, you might have to look back only over the past year. If it's a big decision, you might need to review the past five to ten years. If you're facing a life-altering choice, you might need to take a day and look back over the entire course of your life. If you learn and apply this lesson well, your future will be illuminated.

CHAPTER 18
PURPOSE VS. PASSION
Stop Following the Fleeting

Passions are created by us; purpose is given to us.

Think back over the course of your life about your passions and how they've changed. When I was younger, all I ever wanted to do was one of two things: be a firefighter or a Teenage Mutant Ninja Turtle. Today, I don't have a real interest in doing either. The same principle can be seen in relationships. Take a moment to reflect on your first crush or a relationship where you felt head over heels about the other person, but it has since ended. Your feelings probably aren't described by the word "passionate" anymore, right? We need to review and master this concept internally for our self in order to understand how to use it externally with others.

Passions change, whereas purpose is constant. Passion is volatile, whereas your purpose is stable. Passion is driven from your emotions, whereas purpose is driven by your identity.

Passion and purpose are different in many ways, but the most significant is their source. Passion comes from our desires, our hopes, and our dreams; we get to decide what it is. Purpose, however, comes from a much different place.

Whether you believe it comes from God, the universe, or fate, our purpose in life is something that is given to us from something greater than ourselves. The fastest and most effective way to live a fulfilled life is to take the necessary time to align our passion with our purpose.

I hate walking through the rain, especially when I am not prepared. Before a meeting, after dinner, basically anywhere if I am not prepared, I just hate walking in the rain. Although I hate getting to my car when it's pouring down, frantically trying to avoid puddles and unlock the car at the same time, I do love the instant feeling when I finally get inside my car. It is like I am safe. I am no longer getting drenched by the falling rain. I can still hear it on the hood of my car, but I am safe. I am protected from the elements.

Think about the last time you were outside, and it was raining. I never have an umbrella with me, but I am always grateful when my well-prepared wife tosses me an umbrella from her purse. Although I do not love this experience as much as getting in my car, it is similar because the umbrella is protecting me from the elements. I am on the journey, still working to move forward while staying dry, and the umbrella is helping me fight off the elements. I could still make the walk while the umbrella is held out to the side, but I would be soaked and miserable, whereas if I held the umbrella directly over me, I would feel safe and dry.

Think about purpose like an umbrella. It's there to protect you and keep you moving through the storms. This umbrella is not one you can hold; rather, it is one that is on a consistent path that moves at your speed. Although you cannot direct its path, it keeps pace with you as you walk. Now, your goal is to stay under it if you want its protection. Don't think this limit where you can go. In fact, this umbrella is able to go through the most dangerous and frightening parts of life that you will ever experience. It is during these times that you will need the umbrella the most.

When you take a step, the umbrella follows and protects you—*if* you stay on its path. Remember, you have free will, so you do not need to stay under the umbrella. You have the choice to go wherever you want and chase whatever fleeting desire you see, but when you are outside the umbrella there is little to no protection. Whenever you'd like—and hopefully you are not too far away—you can come back under the umbrella, but again, you cannot change the path of the umbrella. You can only change where *you* go.

Now let's look at passions. These are things we desire through-out life—the things we seek during our walk. They are not always bad—and sometimes they can be particularly good—but here is the realization we need to make. As we said before, your purpose is like this big umbrella that is on a specific path, moving at your speed only when you are under it. Your passions, on the other hand, are ever-changing and all over the place. Some look nice and some look fun, but they are not all good. The biggest thing about passions is that they can be changed, moved, and manipulated by you.

To live a much more fulfilling, simple, and successful life, you should make sure you align your passions and tasks with the umbrella of your purpose. When you know where this umbrella is, it is easy to structure your tasks to be aligned with it. Doing this while life is nothing but sunshine is a huge advantage, but as the "elements" of life start to come your way and make things a bit harder for you, this is when you need to be very deliberate about pulling your passions and tasks under the umbrella. It's like a dog who goes and grabs his favorite bone that is out in the rain and then pulls it into his doghouse to stay dry.

So, here is what I want you to do. Take those movable, ever-changing, volatile passions, and pull them under the umbrella that is your purpose. This will protect you from the elements of life—the change, the fear, the doubt, the hardship, the failure, etc.

When you can bring your passions under your purpose, and not the other way around, you are nearly unstoppable in all of the things you do. When these two concepts are in alignment, your life can continue toward success. However, if your passions don't align with your purpose, you'll live a life full of interruptions and regrets.

Do not waste time trying to figure out what you're passionate about. That is like trying to figure out what candy you like best. Throughout life's many experiences you will find what you like. If you sit down like a kid locked in a candy store and overload yourself by trying everything, eventually you will get sick. Let this part of the journey happen in small doses as you try new things. This is more of a trial-and-error process, not a search for a lost treasure. Now, to find your purpose, that is like searching for a treasure. It will take time and patience, and sometimes you'll need a map. You must be dedicated to the journey and have the patience, but I can offer you a map to help guide you through this expedition. It's the "Why Are You Here" exercise, which you can find online. (https://www.lifepulseinc.com/personal-resources/**why-are-you-here**/) This exercise will help you find your purpose and experience a life where you have an umbrella that can protect you from the elements that in the past have made your journey difficult.

The first thing you need to do is to understand your purpose. As we covered in the last chapter, you do this by reflecting and reviewing your past, not by looking into your desired future. Once you figure out your purpose, begin experimenting with the things you feel passionate about; then see what lines up. When these two are in alignment, you'll see hopes, dreams, and passions become achievements, fulfillment, and successes. This is one of the most critical secrets to living a fulfilled life.

It's easy to let passion become the focus because of the feelings it gives us. Think about Michael Jordan as a young kid. No question,

Michael loved the game of basketball and was passionate about it, but I am sure there were times where he hated practicing. That feeling is forgotten by taking a clutch shot at the end of a game. When we really boil it down, successful people are not necessarily passionate about the individual tasks they perform; they are excited about the feelings they get from completing those actions.

If you're an entrepreneur, you're probably inspired by building your business. If you're in a nonprofit, you might be motivated by helping people. Religious leaders are driven by their relationship with God. Each of these occupations involves tasks aimed in fundamentally different directions, but each is inspired by a sense of success and fulfillment when their individual tasks are completed.

Remember, Passions are related to feelings. You feel good or bad. Your purpose is more tied to your mission. Like our exercise it titled, "Why Are You Here?" Michael Jordan's passion was basketball, but his purpose was much larger than that. You can see proof in that because of all of the things he has done since he stopped playing basketball. Passions are powerful but they can be dangerous when they are not control or contained. These positive feelings you get from following your passions are great but make sure they are protected by being under and in line with your purpose.

Passion is just as fleeting as any other emotion. It is like a match that was just lit. It has the potential to be large and powerful, but the slightest movement of the wind and the match goes out. Once it is gone, the "whatever it takes" mentality that you may have had before seems to go out with it. In the beginning you may need no compensation but when this match is blown out, you will be begging for compensation. Complaining about how it's not "fair" that you do all this hard work without receiving the reward you wanted.

Purpose is what happens when you take that match and you put it towards a gas burner of a stove or a pilot light. Now it can be as weak or powerful as you want but even more importantly, it is consistent. Less ups and down based on external variables. Your Purpose is less about what you get and more about what you're supposed to contribute. When you live under your purpose, passion is the enjoyment you receive from taking the actions. Purpose is external, and passion is internal. When you match these two, your life can actively be fulfilled.

Putting passion before purpose is like following your high school crush to college—it makes sense until reality hits. The key to a fulfilled life is to figure out your purpose and then align your passions with it. Like emotions, your passions change, but the reason you're here doesn't. Passion is created by us, but purpose is given to us. Doing the work to discover your purpose and then using this understanding to guide others through this process will give you the clarity needed to share your purpose with Unmo. Without clarity, Unmo will look right through you as being fake or hypocritical. There is nothing more authentic than living out your purpose.

> **Passions change, but the reason you're here doesn't.**

Once you have found your purpose, you now have a starting point. Too many times we try to take a step forward toward our passion without even thinking about our purpose. We need to have our purpose in our mind with each step we take, which will allow us to take smaller, easier, and more consistent steps in the correct direction.

Then, when an opportunity comes your way, it is much easier to make the right decision to engage or not. I am amazed at how many times I have been able to walk away from what would normally seem like a good idea because it didn't line up with my purpose. Passion-wise, I would have loved to engage, but it didn't line up with my purpose. I have never regretted staying away from something or someone if it went against my purpose.

Our purpose is the ultimate filter to make decisions. If something does not align with your purpose, adjust it to get it to line up with your purpose or disregard it so that it does not distract you. Sometimes the only change something needs is a new frame of reference or a rewording of the task to get it to align with your purpose and motivate you to act.

If you know your purpose, it makes it easy to know where to spend your time and focus, but it also allows you to see each task as connected to a powerful outcome. When we can tie our tasks to our purpose, it is nearly impossible for the Motivation Synapse to degenerate. Identifying why you are here is crucial to being able to self-motivate, which allows us, in turn, to motivate others.

Life is difficult, but somehow, we as humans tend to make it harder than necessary. If you implement this concept of "passion under purpose" in your life, and then help Unmo do the same, you will find that life does not need to feel like that dash to your car on a rainy day: cold, wet, and frustrating.

Find your purpose and use it as an umbrella like we discussed before. Do your best to connect your tasks to your purpose, and you will find passions that you didn't even know you had. Remember, it is your life, so you are more than welcome to focus on passions that are outside of your purpose, but again, that decision is like holding an umbrella out to your side while you walk in the rain. If the umbrella is within your reach, why get wet when you can stay dry? Guide your steps under the umbrella's path, make the walk easy.

YOU - Putting the pieces Together – Post Read

(<u>YOU</u> + Them) x System = Results

The YOU of this system is the most important part. In fact, it is the one part of the system that can be fully controlled by your actions. To master this section, I want you to stick with the following commitments when it comes to each chapter --

Remember, do not be a hypocrite. The second the person you are motivating sees you as anything other than sincere he/she will put up walls that will be difficult for you to overcome. Be you, be honest, and do not try to ask them to do something you would not be willing to yourself.

Part of making sure you are the best version of you is to make sure that you have a healthy balance of influence in your life. That balance comes from who is influencing you and who you are influencing. If you are motiving others, remember, to also ask yourself, who is motivating you? Make sure you have solid influences who can pour into you, so you are able to better pour into others.

With the growth you will experience in perfecting this part of the system, you will need a structure to help keep things moving in the right direction. When we are at our best, we will find that we can do more than even we expect. To avoid becoming overwhelmed and over loaded, live with a 7 days structure. This is where the LP system will support even the most complex life. Ordinary people have a plan when they need it, extraordinary people have a plan before they need it. That is why they can handle more than most even in the most trying times.

As your bandwidth grows and your stress lowers, which this system will help you do, you will want to act and move. Make sure you are A. P.R.O. (Aware, Patient, Ready. and Open) so that when your opportunity comes you can act on it. A commonly used definition of luck is when opportunity meets preparation. Following the steps in this section of the book that you just read will take care of the preparation part of the definition. Being A. P.R.O as discussed will be what allows you to see the opportunity when it comes.

This section is all about YOU. You are the most important person in your life, and I don't mean that you are to put yourself before all others, but you need to take time and continue to discover who you are at all stages of growth. The better you know who you are, the easier it is for you to be confident in who you are. Once you experience this confidence, working with even the most unmotivated people will be a welcome challenge rather than a chore. The way you can support Unmo and your ability to answer questions for Unmo will be simpler once you truly know who you are. Self-awareness is the key to self-confidence. Once you are aware, it makes it much easier to advance.

As you are aware of who you are, and your confidence grows you will find ways to connect with others. Comparison will not be an issue but instead you will be able to relate to others by just being true to who you are. It is like the more you understand yourself the more you know others and you can share (and not compare) the stories that helped make you who you are.

Your focus on being the best version of you will give you the information needed to better predict your future. Most have made the mistake when they are trying to "figure out life" of looking into the future at what it is they want. As we discussed, they key to predicting your future is to review your past. As you get to better know yourself and become more confident in who you are along with what you do, you will be able to see the blue print that has made you who you are as well as the path that will take you to who you are about to become.

Following these steps above leads you to finding your purpose versus endlessly chasing your passions. You will have a confidence in the steps you take each day of your life. Uncovering your purpose and living by your purpose will allow you to handle the elements of life that have thrown you off in the past. It will feel as if challenges will begin to bounce off you rather than hold you down.

So, you have just taken care of the most important, and usually least focused on, portion of this system. You will find once you know you or you are confident in being you, the remaining variables of the formula will be easier to work with. If you do not have a good grasp on who you are and are not authentic in all you do, you will find the other variables of this formula to be exceptionally difficult. The strength of the YOU in this formula could make motivating others enjoyable to do as often as you can, rather than draining. Now that the YOU is under control, enjoy moving to the next step of the system and probably the part of the system you felt needs the most work...THEM. Now that you've read and applied the information in the YOU section, you just made Motivating the Unmotivated much easier than ever before.

KNOWING THEM

For some of you who were not able to be patient, maybe you jumped to this section right away. That is fine; either way, welcome to the "Knowing Them" part of the formula.

Just to reiterate, you can read this section and implement some of these strategies in your relationship with Unmo, but it will be a lot more difficult if you have not worked through the "Knowing You" part first. Also remember, all the teachings in the "Knowing You" part should and could be used by you to help Unmo better understand themselves. One of the hardest parts of motivating the unmotivated is that they rarely know what motivates them. What makes this even harder—and you have probably experienced this in the past—is that "they" don't have a clue what really motivates them. Effective motivators use what is taught in this next section to motivate Unmo, while the best of the best can take lessons in the "Knowing You" chapters to help Unmo find and then self-motivate themselves.

Either way, let's talk about helping Unmo. The first thing we need to realize is that Unmo is not broken, so Unmo does not need to be fixed. You might disagree, but that's just your emotions and ego getting the best of you. Instead of thinking of Unmo as a broken clock, think of Unmo as a clock that just needs to be wound or a guitar that's just a bit out of tune. It's not broken; it just needs to be adjusted a bit.

When motivating "them," we need to meet "them" where they are. Don't throw someone who can't swim into deep water. The result is obvious and not desired. This book will help only if you want to help them swim, not drown them. Tough love has its limits, and once they are surpassed, it is difficult to repair the relationship. If you take one of the most unmotivated individuals and you start pouring down on them all the things you are going to do to "help" them, they will blow you off like they probably already have before. Throwing books at someone who is not going to read them is pointless. Instead, we need to find out where they are and then build them up to where they should be. Then, and only then, can you help build them up to where they could be.

Unmo is only Unmo because they are experiencing a weakened Motivational Synapse between actions and outcomes. This disconnect could be caused by many things. It could be something you've done or something someone else has done. It could be something internal or external about which you have no idea. The key to this section is remembering that you do not know what you do not know, so stop thinking you know and start asking questions to find out!

> *The key to this section is remembering that you do not know what you do not know, so stop thinking you know and start asking questions to find out!*

When working with motivators who are wanting to help motivatees, I have found that all Unmos tend to fall somewhere on this scale. Even some of the best motivators would not be able to properly pin where their Unmo lands, as some biases from the past would interfere. Also, if you asked some Unmos, they would say they are not anywhere on this scale (hence the unaware option). Either way, no matter if you or they can explain where they land, all Unmos can be found somewhere on this scale and lean either one way or the other.

LAZY -- UNAWARE

As the motivator, we tend to quickly put Unmo more toward the lazy category. This is sometimes the case, but not all the time. When we look at it through the lens of the Motivation Synapse, where there is a potential disconnect between the action and the outcome, most Unmos fall more toward the unaware side. They have no clue how unmotivated they are or the implication that has on their current and future life.

What's the big difference if they are lazy or unaware—they are still unmotivated, right? Yes, but the approach we must take as the motivator is much different.

If someone is lazy, that is a choice, and it is a choice they are consciously making. Because being lazy is a choice, they also need to make the choice to no longer be lazy. We cannot make that choice for them. All we can do is help them make that choice. When dealing with someone who is choosing to be lazy, it is a bit more challenging, strictly due to the frustration on your part, but this can be overcome by your mastering the "Knowing You" section and then following the principles detailed in this section ("Knowing Them").

Now if Unmo is unaware, that is a condition, one that usually can be overcome by this section alone (assuming you have yourself in a good place). All we must do is help them be a bit more aware, and if we do that properly most people will go from unmotivated to motivated quickly. We just need to show them the steps they can take to better wed their actions to their desired outcomes.

This is where you, the motivator, comes in. We are tasked with strengthening the Motivational Synapse between action and outcome. Help Unmo understand why sitting on the couch does not help them get the life they say they want, or how showing up late to work is detrimental to the life they want to live. Maybe we need to help Unmo understand why producing at a high level is obviously important for the company, but also why it is important for them.

As we discussed with the Motivation Catalysts that can help bolster this synapse, we need Unmo to see value in the tasks that you want them to complete. Seeing a task as mundane will allow Unmo to approach it like it has little value. If you want to be one of the best motivators for Unmo, the skill sets in this "Knowing Them" section will allow you to do just that.

Special Tip – Two-Minute Drill

Getting this motivational spark started is the hardest part of motivating others. While coaching and training, I suggest to anyone who is having trouble lighting this spark do a Two-Minute Drill. I simply tell them to choose what goal they want to achieve and the action that needs to be taken. All they have to do is commit to do that action for two minutes. Whether it is to read a book, go to the gym, or get on the phone and make prospecting calls, they just have to do it for two minutes and then, if they want, they can stop. As the motivator, we need to celebrate this as a goal accomplished. Even though it is a mere five minutes, it is probably more time than they've spent on it previously. The beautiful thing about this is they can always go over five minutes if they want, and they usually do.

This is the easiest way you can show any motivatee the value behind a task. If they do it consistently, the results will come. If they do it for an hour one day but then do not do it again for weeks or sometimes months, there is little chance to see results despite investing nearly the same amount of time. Even just five minutes each day will produce results.

Try the Two-Minute Drill with yourself, or with Unmo. See how doing ten of these drills over two week, taking the actions, and then going as long or short as you'd like once the first two minutes is up will generate more results than doing one hour every two weeks.

Remember, as you go through this section, you do not know what you do not know, and your entire job is to help Unmo understand the value behind the tasks in which they are taking part. Meet Unmo where they are to help them get where they should be, and then where they could be. And finally, you are sometimes unmotivated as well, so make sure you recognize that being unmotivated is not a character trait; it is a state of mind. Treat Unmo with respect.

> **Meet Unmo where they are to help them get where they should be, and then where they could be.**

CHAPTER 19
THE TYRANNY OF NEGATIVE EXPECTATIONS
Who Rules Who?

Your expectations significantly affect results because they are absorbed by your motivatee.

Let's begin this chapter with an exercise. If you have a piece of paper and a pen, this works best. If not, then you can use your phone. You will need to be able to make two simple lists. Don't just read through this. Write down the answers, and you will see the impact.

Write down the name of the individual you would like to motivate. For most readers, this is the main character of the book, Unmo. I suggest using Unmo if you are nervous of the motivatee seeing this.

Now, forget about yourself for a moment and focus on your motivatee, Unmo; the person in your life you feel is needing motivation. Again, we all have multiple Unmos in our lives, but focus on the one whom you would most like to motivate. You can do this as many times as you want, with as many Unmos as you have, but for now let's start with the hardest Unmo in your life. With this person needing motivation, your answers can range from positive to negative to "I don't know." It is important to understand that this is not what Unmo should do. In order for this to work, you need to write down your honest thoughts about the questions asked. Write your answers under where you wrote the name or moniker of your Unmo. If you're reading this on a Monday or Tuesday, answer the following questions with this week in mind. If it's Wednesday through Sunday, answer them with next week in mind.

1. What is one word that summarizes what Unmo is focusing on for the week?
2. What is Unmo grateful for this week?
3. What are Unmo's goals for the week?

Take some time to write out the answers. Again, it is normal for your answers to range from positive to negative. Some you might not know, and that is fine. The only thing that matters is that you wrote down your honest thoughts related to those questions.

Now let's give Unmo a break for a second and focus on you. Go to a new spot on the page/screen where you can write some more answers. This will be a similar process as before, but this time put your name at the top and give yourself room to answer three questions about you. Write your answers to all three before moving on.

1. What is one word that summarizes what you are focusing on for the week?
2. What are you grateful for the week?
3. What are your goals for the week?

There are only three ways you could respond: a positive answer, a negative answer, or an "I don't know." If you do not know the answers to these questions, that is fine, but in order to sustainably motivate your motivatee, knowing their answers will make the whole process not only more bearable, but also more enjoyable for both parties. The best way to find out the answer to these questions is simply by asking them or making sure these questions are intertwined in whatever system you decide to use to motivate the unmotivated.

Most people find their answers for Unmo were more negative and assuming compared to the responses for themselves. Or some people didn't want to be negative, so they wrote "nicer" comments about Unmo than they naturally thought. Expectations of Unmo need to be fair, but for most they are probably lower, more negative, and often fatalistic. Remember, this Unmo is the unmotivated person in your life and has probably given you good reason to have these negative thoughts, so it is no surprise that they are surfacing in this exercise.

When you compare your responses about Unmo to how you answered the questions for yourself, you probably are a bit more optimistic about yourself: you had focus, you were grateful, and you had goals. You might not have been able to answer right away, but you passionately believed that you could answer those questions. It's human nature to have a positive outlook on ourselves, but we need to give an even and fair evaluation to Unmo—not just because it is the right thing to do, but because it is the only way to get an accurate understanding of where Unmo is and how you can help them get to where they should be. If we are biased in a positive way for ourselves, we could choose to be biased in a positive way toward Unmo. Although it is better for our expectation of Unmo to tend more toward the positive rather than the negative, neither is the goal. The goal here is the truth.

I understand that the negative thoughts that popped into your head were probably warranted. They are likely based on a series of experiences you have had with Unmo where they've let you down. However, their actions are driven by their expectations of themselves, and

> **While positive expectations don't guarantee success, negative expectations often ensure failure.**

those expectations are profoundly influenced by yours. While positive expectations don't guarantee success, negative expectations often ensure failure.

This exercise is part of a structure we use at Life Pulse, and we've applied it in business settings that vary from small startups to Fortune 500 companies. The same system can be used in family or relational environments.

We were working with a manufacturing company that had employees ranging from six-figure salary earners to hourly contractors. When I had the CEO complete this exercise, he identified certain people as potential troublemakers who would fight any system we tried to put in place. Not surprisingly, he was right, and we encountered resistance. I wanted to understand how his expectations fit into the picture, so I had him complete this task with one of the "problem" employees in mind.

The CEO's "one-word focus" that he chose for this employee (Unmo) was negative. He felt Unmo was lacking gratitude for anything and had no real goals. When we went to the employee and asked for his results, the CEO was shocked. He had a positive and intentional one-word focus. The employee was grateful for his religious beliefs, which the CEO shared but never knew they had in common. Unmo had a series of goals, including his continued success as a coach for a youth sports team that had made it to the state championships. He was a father and was passionate about coaching his children, who were on the team.

The CEO hadn't seen any of this. When he looked at his employee, he had only negative expectations. The executive realized that his thought processes toward his subordinate would never have allowed the employee to succeed. Walking through this exercise helped the two of them connect and create a better working relationship than they'd ever had before. Nothing changed in their tasks or responsibilities, but the interaction between the two changed instantly. The understanding they now had of each other changed the trajectory of the relationship and, because of that, the results at work.

We did the same thing with a father and son and experienced similar results. The dad had a negative attitude toward his son. He didn't think his son had goals or gratitude, and he had no faith that his son was going anywhere. When he realized how harmful his thought processes were, he went through the LP each week with his son. . Now, he and his son meet on a weekly basis, and the father is consistently surprised at what his son is focusing on, grateful for, and the kinds of goals he's making. The son has gone from someone who couldn't succeed to being far more self-managed, and he is beginning to rack up achievements.

Complete this exercise with anyone you identify as a motivatee, even if you would not characterize them as "unmotivated," and ask them to do the same so you can see their results. You want to develop a positive image in your mind of how they operate so that you can change your expectations and create an environment that will allow them to be successful. Remember, positive expectations don't guarantee success, but negative expectations often ensure failure.

CHAPTER 20
MOTIVATIONAL WALLS
The Walls We Build That We Must Break Down

The walls we build are sometimes the hardest walls to tear down.

As you've read, the business concept of "value proposition" is a term that will help us understand the Motivational Proposition, or "M-Prop" as we've called it, that motivates others. Sellers motivate buyers to purchase something by showing them the value they'll receive from it. If there's no value, there's no reason the buyer would consider getting it. When you want to motivate someone, focusing on how they will win as a result of the situation is critical. Humans naturally want to win; we want to succeed, and we want to be fulfilled. Understanding the link between any individual action and that victory is crucial.

Some of the best examples of this can be found in sales and marketing. People decide to buy something to do one of two things: experience pleasure or avoid pain. The best sales and marketing professionals can instantly connect this synapse between buying (action) and outcome (experience pleasure/avoid pain). Next time you are watching a commercial or see an ad, catch yourself when you think, "Hmm, I might need that." BOOM, that is when they got you. That is the instant that your walls have come down, and they have strengthened the synapse to help you make the decision to buy what they are selling. Motivation for actions beyond purchasing works in the same way.

Walls are built to protect us. One wall we all know of is the Great Wall of China, which was built during the Ming Dynasty to protect the Chinese Empire from the Mongolians and other invaders. At nearly 4,000 miles long, we can all agree that it is a big wall with a big purpose: to protect and keep out invaders. Our brains tend to have walls with the same purpose—not as long, but possibly more powerful, as once these walls go up it is difficult for us to bring them down.

The human brain is a Wonder of the World on its own. Its abilities and processing power are unlike anything else on this planet. With all we know about how our brain works, there is still so much to find out. One thing we do know is that our brains are made of three distinct parts that work together in perfect harmony. The first is referred to as the "Old Brain." I call this the "Frogger Brain" in honor of the old arcade game where you had to jump across a highway without getting hit. The goal of the game was survival— and that's the focus of the Old Brain too.

This is the first barrier we face when trying to motivate someone else. When we ask people to do something, the first subconscious thought is: "Will this kill me?" Or, another way to think of it: "How could this negatively impact me?"

The more trust and rapport you've built with someone, the lower that barrier will be, because they know you have only their best interests at heart. If your motivatee doesn't know you well, the wall will be high. If you've harmed someone in the past, that wall can sometimes feel like the size of an entire skyscraper. Both can be overcome, but the effort is much different based on the size of the wall in place. Sometimes we built this wall for Unmo. Sometimes Unmo has built this wall themselves. And sometimes the walls are built by Unmo's experiences outside of either of your control. It is hard to always know what causes these walls to be built up, but instead of focusing on how they were built, we need to focus on how we can help Unmo break them down.

When we ask for something from Unmo, each section of the brain has its own walls to filter this request. Some walls quickly drop, and some stand strong like the Great Wall of China. Let's say you make a simple request to Unmo. Even if you receive an instant response, all requests go through the same path. First, it encounters Unmo's Old Brain. Then it is sent to be processed by the second part: the "Midbrain." I call this the "Filter Brain" because the mind's goal here is to filter through the immediate request and understand the meaning of what is being said. Only at this second level of the brain are you able to reason and have complex thoughts. The Old Brain (Frogger) has decided that the request isn't going to kill them, and the Midbrain (Filter) can enter a complex cost/benefit analysis. Of course, there can still be walls around the Filter Brain, but there are some inputs that we as the motivators can offer to help bring down these walls.

Finally, the request moves onto the third part of the thought process, the "Neocortex," which I refer to as the "Solution Brain." This is where you problem-solve and come to a solution or decision. It is where a request needs to arrive to allow motivation to be a simple task we can implement and receive.

Walls around the Frogger Brain can be tough, as they deal with yes-or-no decisions. No logic or reason—just fight or flight. These walls will always be the hardest to bring down if they exist. Walls around the Frogger Brain are built to keep people out. Walls around the Filter Brain are still large, but it is like it has a door that you can knock. Someone will let you in as long as they don't think you will kill them. Then the wall of the Solution Brain is like property lines that you and your neighbor agree on; you still need permission if you are to cross them, but this permission usually is granted if your neighbor (Unmo) thinks you have a good enough explanation.

All three parts of the brain have walls, and that is healthy as the walls are meant to protect us. However, these walls tend to keep the motivator from helping Unmo strengthen the synapse. It is like Unmo would rather keep you out and stay safe than let you in to help them. They need to trust you are safe before they let you behind their walls. Everyone has these walls that are not physical in nature but rather are built on fear—fears of things like heights, snakes, and spiders, or less tangible things such as rejection or failure.

Let's use my friend Brian's fear of heights as an example. If Brian and I went hiking up a steep mountain with a group of friends, we might arrive at the face of a cliff. While the rest of us would walk straight to the edge and look over without hesitation, Brian would require quite a bit of coaxing. If he mustered the courage to do this, and I, as a bad friend, pretended to push him, the stimulus would immediately cause walls to form around all three parts of the brain, like multiple doors closing a highly protected vault. Now we have a lot of work to do to get back in. If the Frogger Brain could talk, it would shout, "They're trying to kill you!" and Brian would grab anything he could in an attempt to save his life.

Once he felt secure, or at least like he wasn't going to die, the Filter Brain would try to process what just happened. *Did my friend just try to kill me, and I survived? Was he trying to mess with me?* When he realized what I did was a poor attempt at humor, his Solution Brain would then creatively approach the situation and determine whether he should laugh with me or punch me in the face.

When motivatees overcome their walls, it is like they conquered a mountain. It is not easy and can even be terrifying at times. When they overcome the wall, recognize that just because they let it down once, it could very well still be there. It is also possible, but unlikely, that the wall could come back stronger. Remember, these walls are here to keep you out. That is the entire role of the wall. If you help build the wall, you are just making it harder to get in. However, if you help them overcome the wall, you will rarely have to experience that wall in the future, at least not at full intensity like before.

The long-term repercussions of my actions, however, are enormous. How do you think Brian will react the next time I ask him to do something that makes him uncomfortable? Do you think there's even a chance he'll consider it? I've just encouraged him to create a Motivational Wall, and that two seconds of immature humor might take years to overcome.

Think about someone you don't trust, then consider the reason why that is. Tearing walls down takes far longer than it takes to put them up. The only way it can happen is by practicing complete transparency as you rebuild trust.

When you're trying to motivate someone, you not only need to show them the value of doing what you're asking; you need to understand the role and existence of Motivational Walls. Motivational Walls are caused by many things, as explored above, but we need to be careful that we are not helping build or reinforce these walls. Walls are built up by the motivator when one of two things happens: either you are speaking truth to the motivatee and it is colliding with a wound of theirs, or you are speaking from a wound of yours, which is then combined with a wound of theirs. Avoiding creating Motivational Walls in others is crucial, so we must always be aware of the difference between intent and impact. The former is what action we meant to do, and the latter is what that action produced.

Building these walls is like adding hurdles to a marathon. Convincing someone to run a marathon is challenging enough;

adding obstacles they have to overcome makes it nearly impossible. Trying to motivate from fear or power is almost guaranteed to result in walls being built. Motivating based on love and understanding is the opposite of this. Sometimes we think that the fastest way to get someone to do something is to force them to. In reality, this can be a quick way to create action, but it is often the slowest way to get sustainable results.

The bigger the walls someone has, the more time and patience are required to break them down. However, if you want long-lasting, sustainable results with your motivatee and are willing to put in the time and effort to make it happen, the ROI on your investment is virtually endless.

Unmo has this weakened Motivation Synapse between action and outcome. These walls are built in between these gaps, making it nearly impossible for the two to connect. When this happens, we need to stop desperately trying to run our head through the wall in order to bring it down. Instead, back up; ask the right questions to the person who has the wall, and you will see the wall come crumbling down. You will see more of this in the SYSTEM part of the book.

Not all of the walls are seen by you, the motivator, as not all of the walls are even seen by them. So, if you are struggling to motivate someone, either one of two things are happening: either you are doing a bad job of communicating, or they are not receiving your communication. If you are sure you are doing your part and they just aren't receiving it, that is when we know there is a Motivational Wall blocking the possible connection between their action and outcome.

We need to understand that if there is a wall there, we need to first start working on bringing that wall down. The best way to do this is by understanding what is causing that wall to stay up. Once this is identified, growth must occur while avoiding the triggers at all cost. This seems like a lot of work on your part, as a motivator, but by doing this now you will save yourself a lot of time and energy in the future.

Taking time to ask some questions from previous chapters is a good first step. But the most important thing to do is to get to know what they like, who they are, and what their story is. The more I know about someone, the easier it is for me to motivate them. This is not just because of the knowledge I now have of them but how I use the knowledge to better lead them.

I take what they have experienced and combine this with the interests they have. With this information in my arsenal, I can help them determine what needs to be done. As motivators, we must connect the dots for our motivatees once we know their information. How do we take what they love and give them more of this? How do we help them avoid what has built up their walls going forward? This is how we connect the dots.

There is a common theme here: we need to connect actions to outcomes, but without bringing down a person's walls this task only slips further away from our grasp. To break down these walls, we need to find their root source and the person hiding within them. We need to show (not tell) the motivatee that they do not need to protect themselves from you. It does not matter what, or who, caused these walls to be built; it is our responsibility to help break them down. Through love and understanding, we can get more of what they want and avoid what they don't want.

As we break down these walls and motivate those around us, it sometimes feels like improv comedy. Some people have taken improv classes to enhance their business skills because improv can teach us great lessons about reacting in the moment. In improv, the primary objective is to keep the joke moving forward. In motivation, the main goal is keeping your motivatee moving forward. Seek understanding of where they are coming from and what they are struggling with and feeling. Ask clarifying questions to get to the root of the matter. The more you understand your motivatee, the stronger the relationship and the better your results.

Look back at the walls you might have built with Unmo. Even if they were not your fault, they are still your responsibility if you want to motivate Unmo. How can we pull those walls down? Start by asking more questions about what they want and what they don't want. The goal is to offer your motivatees things that are beneficial to them. Genuinely desire a positive result. Remember that if you try to manipulate them into a bad decision, you'll be able to do it only once. Connect the dots; show the motivatee that they are significant and involved in something bigger than the walls that have been built. I promise you will see consistent results!

CHAPTER 21
BEING VS. TELLING
We Can't Hear You over the Nonsense

The best way to motivate someone is through being, not telling.

At the beginning of the book, I wrote about the two primary ways to motivate people: fear and love. The former is a short-term impact that stops the moment it is no longer being applied. The latter is a long-term mechanism that continues to inspire action long after it is shown. It is like putting pressure on an open cut. Fear is a Band-Aid; love is the suture.

Fear is a Band-Aid; love is the suture.

Think of some of the people who have changed history: Mother Teresa, Mahatma Gandhi, Princess Diana, Martin Luther King Jr., and Jesus Christ. At their very core, what they all had in common was authenticity. Their power came from who they were, not what they said. In fact, many of the things they said weren't laboriously prepared speeches or books that had been edited and revised for years on end. Their remarks were often off the cuff and stated from the heart. Their most quotable moments were honest reflections of who they were in their very essence. Rather than just telling people what to do, they showed people how to live.

People who are great motivators are motivated themselves. As I've mentioned before, it's virtually impossible for me to be positively motivated to earn more money by someone who is Has no money, or to get in shape by someone who is in poor health. These people might have all the knowledge in the world, and they might know all the right things to say. But in the end, if they don't live the life that shows the results people are seeking, be careful to jump behind them and follow.

We have a list of the Top Motivators that we consider "Motivational All-Stars." Again, we do not consider someone who uses fear as a "good" motivator. Anyone can scare others into action. These are people who did a fantastic job motivating individuals because of their authenticity. You might not agree with their beliefs or positions, but you should focus on why they inspired others. These are the five things they tend to have in common:

1. **Genuine care for people:** The best motivators don't work off manipulation but genuinely care about their followers as much or more than the outcome.
2. **Living Proof:** They live what they teach and have been doing it for quite a while. The proof is in their story.
3. **Unwavering faith:** Their experiences have given them a foundation that is virtually unbreakable. They might have gone through some incredibly tough times but making it through them has convinced them of their beliefs.
4. **Patience to do the right thing:** They can bear trials calmly or without complaint, manifest forbearance under strain, avoid acting hastily or impetuously, and remain steadfast despite opposition. Patience isn't just sitting back and doing nothing—it's lasting through trials without knowing what the outcome will be.
5. **Simple ideas that are universally applicable:** They knew that the secret wasn't found in having a profound, groundbreaking, earth-shaking discovery, but rather that the essence of motivating others lay in connecting with people.

Imagine living a life where you could always use yourself as an example. This doesn't mean that you're perfect, but it does mean that you can live your life so authentically that when you speak about the things you'd like to see accomplished, it comes from the heart and people know that you truly believe, to your core, what you're talking about. This is one reason why the "Knowing You" section of this book is so important for everyone to read. If you can find and be the authentic YOU, then people will be more likely to follow your lead.

> *Patience isn't just sitting back and doing nothing—it's lasting through trials without knowing what the outcome will be.*

A mentor once told me that I needed to spend more time living the principles I taught and less time preparing what I had to say. In doing this, teaching, and leading became simple. There was little to no need to prepare as I ended up with more stories than I had time to tell. It didn't matter if I was training one on one, speaking to my company, or speaking in front of thousands of people, I was just telling my story, so it was easy to lead and even easier for them to listen.

If you want someone to be more motivated, become more motivated yourself. If you want them to be more productive, become more productive in your own life. The same can be said for being kind, or being a team player, or any other quality you'd like to see developed in others. It starts with you.

Assume that you've been tasked with motivating or inspiring others to live by positive principles throughout their life. Instead of creating a PowerPoint full of others' quotes or studies as to why they should do what you are saying, try this...

Take a few minutes and write out what you'd like to say. Review your list; then commit to living by those principles for a month. Once you have experienced what it's like to truly live out those principles, you will find that others with whom you interact will start to act differently as well. It is not automatic, and most of the time it takes longer than we would like, but you'll see not only a positive change in yourself but also incremental improvements in the way those around you act. If you then get the chance to use words, simply tell them your story. You will be amazed how easy and effective this is!

It reminds me of the first time I spoke professionally. Usually, most speakers getting started would look to do a short talk and then get off stage before anyone threw tomatoes. Not me—for some reason I said I wanted to do a full workshop on how to use our LP system. I called it "Life Planning for Entrepreneurs" and was given three hours to fill. The problem was, I had not ever given this workshop before, nor had I even created it. We didn't even have a company yet. We just had a little blue book that transformed our life, but we had no idea how much it could help others. . So when I came home and told Maria about the workshop I had agreed to do—and very soon—she very calmly took a deep breath and said, "Matt, I love you and believe in you, but what are you going to talk about for three hours?!"

I had no answer at the time, but I knew that I had lived enough life, with enough positive and negative experiences, to make it worth it to the audience to stay for three hours. I would challenge you that no matter how old or young you are, no matter how easy or hard your life has been, you do too. You can do exactly as I did. To help, I went to Maria and said, "I need your help to pull out stories of our life that could help illustrate how this works." The key to this part is authenticity and not just making up or embellishing stories. We need to pull these from our past. And remember, it does not matter how dramatic or heart-wrenching the results are; it must simply reflect how we have lived our lives.

If you have lived an ongoing life of disorganization, procrastination, or demotivation, then your first step is to go back and work on you. Like I said before, take some time to experience what life is like when you practice what you preach, and you will find it makes "preaching" a lot easier. If you are in a position where you are responsible to motivate another human, I would assume that you have done something in your life that you could share with the motivatee to help articulate your desired goal.

Remember, the best motivators enhance engagement by being rather than telling. When you are telling, you are saying things like "You should..." but when you are being, you will be saying things like "I did..." People like hearing what you did much more than hearing what they should be doing, so stop "shoulding" on people.

I sat down and wrote out all the talking points that I wanted to get across to the audience—the main points as to how and why we built the LP system the way we did. Initially, there was a lot of what the audience should do. My goal when speaking is the same when motivating catch myself when I hear myself say "You should" and instead tell a story. As we went through all of the parts, Maria and I said, "What stories did we experience that we can share?" It took some time to get going, but eventually we had to start cutting out stories because we had too much content.

I realized this works when speaking to crowds, it works when speaking to companies, and it works when speaking to customers. I had to think of what it was I wanted to get across and then think of stories that backed that claim. Again, no embellishing—only true stories.

Think about the last time you heard a good story. It could be a speech, movie, book, podcast, etc. You likely connected to it because it resonated with who you are and what you have been through. People remember stories over facts. People want to relate to the people they are being motivated by. If you can take the time, not to prep the perfect sales pitch, but to think of the perfect story you can tell the motivatee so that they can understand the value of what you are asking them to do, the motivation will stick with them long after you are in their presence.

The only preparation you need to properly motivate someone is the ability to connect the point you are trying to get across with an experience in your life. Take time to think about your life, the experiences you have had, and how can you open yourself up to share that story to help you motivate the unmotivated. Be the person you want others to be then let them see from your lifestyle how they can better themselves. By doing this properly, you will need less words, as the person you are will speak louder than the words you are saying. Don't be surprised if people start changing around you without your saying much. Be a walking reminder of whom they should strive to be.

CHAPTER 22
PROVIDING A PURPOSE VEHICLE
Can You Get Me from Point A to Point B?

When people know where they want to go, how they get there is of little concern.

"The future of your organization and the potential of your employees are intertwined; their destinies are linked."[22]

That's a quote from the book *Dream Manager* by Matthew Kelly and is one that has stuck with me for years. This book was the one that unlocked my understanding there is a positive way to motivate outside of force-based motivation.

Dream Manager tells the story of a small janitorial company called Admiral Janitorial Services and the general manager, Simon Roberts. The GM's biggest problem was turnover, which had hit a high of 400 percent. No one would stay with the company for more than a year, and most positions rotated employees four or five times over a mere twelve months.

Roberts knew that if he sat down with company leadership and tried to get to the bottom of the problem, the best they would be able to come up with would be educated guesses. He wasn't satisfied with that, so he went straight to the source: the employees themselves. He asked them what they wanted out of life, and

---

[22] Matthew Kelly, *The Dream Manager* (New York: Hyperion, 2007), 1.

the goals were different for each person. One person was saving for a new car, while another wanted to take his family on a cruise. Roberts realized that few people wake up in the morning motivated to do janitorial tasks, so he decided to switch the company's focus from putting janitorial success at the forefront to emphasizing doing what was right for their employees as the number one goal.

Within a year, the turnover had been cut in half. What they also found was that sick days decreased by nearly a third and tardiness dropped by two-thirds. Employees weren't just staying with the company; they were doing a much better job while they were there. The concept of the "Dream Manager" was born, and a person in that role became focused on finding out what employees wanted and making it happen. When the company used that approach, it flourished.

Stick with me for this one, as I am going to introduce some terms you might not have heard before. Whether you manage hundreds of employees or don't have a single direct subordinate, wanting to motivate a family member, or a peer you can begin to apply this principle. When a job becomes a vehicle to achieve a dream rather than the goal itself, people start to buy into the organization's purpose. When a child recognizes that they have responsibilities to the family, they will start contributing. When your pet realizes there is value in waiting to go outside and go to the bathroom, they will start obeying. That is why we call this means to an end the "Purpose Vehicle." When renting a vehicle, your primary desire is getting to the destination. You do not care so much about it being the vehicle of your dreams. Focus on what is desired then you will see there are many options of vehicles you and your motivatee can take. In fact, in most cases, whatever "vehicle" they are currently using, could easily allow them to live out their purpose.

It can be their job or the task you want them to complete, but either way, as a motivator and as we have said before, you want the motivatee to connect value to each task. You want them to be connected to the task. This happens when there is PVTT, or Personal Value Tied to Task. If they don't see value it will be difficult for them to connect action to outcome.

Sometimes what we want to do with our lives lines up perfectly with the job we have and going to work every day is an absolute joy. More often than not, however, we go to work because we have to. When we shift the focus from the job being the end and instead look at it as a means, with our dreams and desires as the primary focus, we become much more effective at our job.

I am sure you or someone you know has experienced the pinball effect in their career. This is when someone bounces from job to job and can't seem to hold on to any job. Sometimes this is related to their competence, but for a competent person more often it occurs because they are not able to see how the job is a Purpose Vehicle that can get them what they really want out of life.

I feel terrible when I meet people who leave a good job because they want to follow their passion, or they think they are just wasting their life at their current job. Anyone who feels that way is hurting because their identity—and the only identity they can see for themselves—is in that job. As motivators, we need to let the motivatee see how that job can help them get where they want, which will strengthen the synapse connecting action and outcome. In the example above, the focus was not on janitorial success but instead on recognizing that if an employee did their job, they could save up and take their family on the cruise they have always wanted. Focusing on the fun and excitement of a cruise with your family (depending on the family) is a lot more motivating and energizing than scrubbing the inside of a toilet.

Sometimes the synapse is so weakened that you need to change Unmo's focus from what they get as a result to what they get FROM the result (or what they can do with the result they get). It reminds me of when I am traveling to visit a client and I need to get a rental car. The only reason you get a rental car is to get from point A to point B. The outcome is you get to point B, but the true value of getting to point B is what you get to do once you are there. Once at point B, I can connect with a client. Maybe for Unmo getting to point B will allow them to take the trip they wanted or maybe just give them a chance to relax. There is an outcome you get, and then there is a result you get to experience because you got to point B.

When traveling to see a client, I only need to get in the car and drive to get this experience. What I do not need to do is shop around the lot to see which Nissan Versa I would rather take. If there is a selection, feel free to waste your time shopping around, but if you need to get from point A to point B, you make the most of what you are given. This is not a message to settle for whatever life throws your way; it is a message that you and Unmo do not need to worry about what vehicle gets you from A to B. Instead, focus on what you will get to experience once you arrive at point B. When the actions and results are known and constantly focused on, the actions make sense. You wouldn't even mind showing up in a clown car because all you care about is safely getting to point B (outcome).

Unless you are in a career in which the task itself is tied directly to your purpose in life, you will always feel a bit disconnected until you design how your current position is a Purpose Vehicle for you. Whatever you or Unmo currently do in life, your goal is to find a way to connect it with our or their purpose. There may be a simple connection, or you might have to get creative. Using an exercise similar to our "Why Are You Here?" that helps discover your purpose, will give a clear answer. In the rare case that there is just no way to connect what is being done with the discovered purpose, then maybe it is time for a change. Before you give up on this step, because our true purpose is so broad and never tied to any specific task or assignment, you most likely can find a way for the current position to be one of the many Purpose Vehicles that may be used to experience the desired ideal life.

When it comes to motivating Unmo, knowing where they want to go and what they want in life is the most powerful information you can have. As motivators, all we need to do is make sure Unmo is aware that what they are doing (business, school, tasks, etc.) is just a Purpose Vehicle. Instead of them feeling "used" by these tasks that seem mundane, we need to help them see how they can flip the script and start using these tasks as a vehicle to get to what they want.

This can be difficult and take some creativity on your part, but the constant reminder of where they truly want to be and what they truly want to get out of life could help them not only make it through but thrive while completing these tasks. If they are grinding out an hourly job to pay for something they really want or to take their family on a trip, stop reminding them to do the boring tasks that they cannot connect with their desires. Instead, help them recognize that every small, seemingly point-less task is taking them one step closer to getting what they really want. So, to do this we need to get to know our motivatee, asking them questions about what they want out of life and then helping them understand how doing these tasks now can help them get what they want in the future.

Make it your goal to find the dream destination for you and your motivatee. Once you've discovered this, you can select the best Purpose Vehicle to get there and make sure they understand their PVTT (Personal Value Tied to Task). If you can do this, you will easily overcome any Motivational Walls and quickly strengthen the Motivational Synapse. When you're working with other people, don't make assumptions: don't assume they want what you want. Find out what makes them tick, and then work with them so that the tasks you have them doing help them get to their dream destination.

CHAPTER 23
HOW TO HERD CATS
Slippery Little Things

The easiest way to herd cats is to move the food bowl. Offer them something they want, and they will find a way to get it.

My business was running smoothly; we had millions of dollars in sales, and the operational systems were nearly automatic. I had some free time, so I decided to pick up a hobby. I had just finished reading a book called *I Can Fix America: 52 common sense ways YOU can make the United States great again* that advised implementing one new habit every week in your own life and taking personal responsibility for how your actions contribute to the nation's health. This seemed as good a place to start as any, so I tried to implement the first habit: buy local.

This was far harder than I could have imagined. After a few weeks of trying to do this, I realized that virtually no one in the area offered local products. A crazy idea slowly formed in my mind: What if I could help farmers sell to big-box stores? The concept of Local Vendors Coalition (LVC) was developed.

I needed to talk to the largest grocery store in the area and find out why they weren't buying local. I got on a freelancing website, had a logo made for $20, created this image on PowerPoint, printed it out on an 8.5" x 11" piece of paper, and pitched my idea to the largest national grocer at that time:

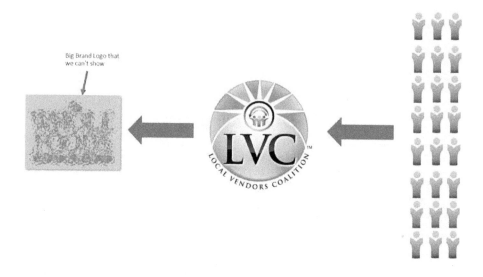

I walked in, went straight up to customer service, and asked to speak to whomever was in charge of buying produce. Right as she was asking if I had an appointment (which I didn't), the produce buyer walked by. Out of what was most likely a mixture of sympathy and curiosity, he agreed to speak with me. I showed him my business plan, the piece of paper with the image above, and he laughed. Undeterred, I asked him: "If I could get product of the same or higher quality, for the same or lower prices, from local farmers, would you be interested?" He said he would, and the business was born.

The next step was getting in touch with the farmers, and this proved to be far more difficult than I thought. I tried calling, texting, and e-mailing, but no one would answer or respond. I was frustrated and disheartened. Finally, on my last call one night, a farmer picked up. I vented to him and said, "Man, you farmers are hard to get a hold of. Trying to get in touch with you is like herding cats."

In a thick Southern drawl, the farmer responded: "Boy, you want to learn something real' quick?" At this point, I was a bit nervous. The last time a farmer asked me this, he followed it up by telling me that I was full of piss and vinegar, which apparently is not a compliment, but it made sense to me once I looked it up. I reluctantly agreed, and the farmer said: "Herding cats is simple—just move the food bowl."

Over the next few days, I tried to figure out how to apply that simple lesson. I kept attempting to get in touch with farmers and finally made my first purchase from someone: a bushel of peppers and a bushel of cucumbers. I sold that to the big box store for $31.26, but between the truck rental, gas, and insurance, the trip cost me more than $500. This wasn't going to work.

Then something funny happened. I had apparently moved the food bowl. When I placed that first check in the farmer's hands, he realized I was serious. Suddenly, they started trying to get in touch with *me*. Although the farmers had said they wanted more outlets for their products, their actions didn't match that. The reason was simple: they needed to see results before they would change. I kept trying to sell them the big dream, and they've heard it all before. They wanted to actually see the results. I gave them the proof, and their entire outlook shifted. I found out what it was they wanted to eat and gave them as much as I possibly could. The more checks I got in their hands, the more they wanted to work with us!

Human performance is an interesting thing. When people have too little to do or it's boring, uninteresting work, they don't achieve everything they can. It is like they are not interested in the food you have served them to eat, so they decide not to eat at all. Serving someone food they don't like will never excite them. They may eat it out of respect to you, but eventually if you keep forcing it on them, they will start to push back.

The sweet spot for performance comes when someone has a full plate—not overflowing with "food" but with just the right amount to satisfy Unmo's appetite and confirm your faith in them. If a food bowl or plate is out of reach, they will never bother reaching for it. If it is too easy to get, they might overindulge. The goal is to give them just enough to satisfy their appetite but not overstuff them to the point of being in a food coma on the couch. We want Unmo to be continuously stimulated, rewarded when they get to the plate, and purposefully not overfed, causing overwhelm. You can see this principle illustrated graphically in the following chart:

Remember that this optimum performance level is different for each person. One of the consistent themes in this book has been getting to know yourself and your motivatee before attempting to offer any solutions. Your optimum performance might be higher, or lower, than someone else's.

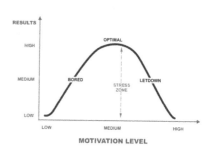

This is why motivation is such an important concept, because when people drive themselves, they are able to do *their* best work effectively and efficiently. Imagine a day where Unmo becomes self-motivated. It is like the day your child can finally get food for themselves. They can now survive on their own, and you can guide as needed, versus just being needed!

This concept of herding cats by moving the food bowl was stuck in my head. And when I heard it, I realized I have tried multiple times to move to food bowl. There were two reasons they weren't "coming to eat." First was

I wasn't putting the right food in the bowl. It wasn't something they wanted. Secondly was the placement of the bowl. It was either too far out of their reach or to close where there was no effort needed on their side. Remember, it is not just what you food you discover needs to be in the bowl (i.e. motivation catalyst), but it is also important to make sure the position of the bowl is exactly where it should be. When looking at the chart, you will see that there is a level at the top of the bell curve representing optimum performance. Getting someone there is as easy as placing the food bowl right there.

If you want to see growth in your motivatee, move the food bowl a bit to the right. I think back to when I met with a client who became a good friend and a mentor of mine, Dr. Kofi Smith. Kofi had recently been named Atlanta's Most Admired CEO, and he sat down and drew this out on a napkin for me. He calls it the SIP, or "Strategic Inflection Point." It was based on something he learned while in school, but the way he uses it to motivate his team and himself is spectacular. I am hoping when he writes his book, this concept is a part of it because of the impact it has made on the way I manage others.

When Unmo is on an upward trajectory, Kofi already has their next bell curve ready, resetting the trajectory as soon as they get to the top of the curve. For some of the most motivated individuals, you can reset the trajectory right as they hit the apex of the curve. For others, they need some time to enjoy the accomplishment. Either is fine, but make sure you are offering the next curve at the SIP before they start falling over the edge.

Eventually, we need to redraw the curve. If I keep moving the food bowl to the right without growing my motivatee, you pass the stress zone and your motivatee will start feeling

more anxious or defeated. Because of that they will tend to stop doing what is needed and you will start seeing diminishing returns or the "let down" part of the curve. As we redraw the trajectory, we need to make sure we are still serving the right food and checking that the food bowl is in the best possible placement—right at the apex, "right after the stress zone".

The optimum area for growth is right in front of the stress zone. Athletes know that if you want to improve your performance, you need to stress your muscles. The same is true in every other area of life. You don't want to cross into the anxious zone, but if you find the sweet spot just before it, adaptation and growth will heighten. This isn't a technique to trick or manipulate your motivatees. When you do this with *their* best interests in mind, your goal is always their success. You want them to grow, develop, and achieve more.

Remember, it isn't our job to help our motivatees get what WE want—it's our job to help them achieve what THEY want. Be a mentor, a sounding board, and a coach, rather than a dictator. Help your motivatees see the value (PVTT) in the tasks they're assigned.

This takes patience. Sometimes you'll give what you think is wise advice and get frustrated when people ignore it. When this happens, take a moment to calm down. Remember that you haven't always embraced the advice others have given you. Remember that this is *their* journey, not yours, and you need to be focused on helping them along, rather than forcing them to go where you want. True motivators understand their job is to share... not save.

Know what your motivatees want in the food bowl. Make sure you are serving them food they want to eat, as you are working to give your motivatee what *they* want and not what *you* want. Find the location of the food bowl and understand how you can move it to help the motivatee get what they want. If the food bowl is in the correct spot on the chart to achieve optimum performance or growth, fill it with the food your motivatee wants. They will instantly become motivated, and your role as slave driver is a distant memory! Instead, you can be that sounding board, or mentor, that you would probably rather be.

CHAPTER 24
I DIDN'T TAKE YOUR PARKING SPOT TODAY
Why Communication Is So Hard

Communication is taking an emotional thought and trying to articulate it through logic.

A primary element of motivation is communication, and communication is tough. This is because we humans are emotionally charged beings, and communication is an attempt to take deep, complicated emotions and put them into words. When you look up "love" in the dictionary, for example, you'll find ten separate meanings. Differentiating between them is entirely contextual.

If you have ever read any book on communication or taken a course on the subject, you would know that 93 percent of our communication isn't even comprised of the words we use. Body language, facial expressions, and vocal intonation all play a crucial role in telling our listeners precisely what we're trying to say.

As efficient as electronic communication has made sending words, it's made genuine communication much more difficult. Writing things down for internal use is massively beneficial, but when we are communicating through the written word, we lose 93 percent of our message. According to a study by Radicati Group, more than 205 billion e-mails were sent *daily* in 2015, and that number was expected to easily exceed 246 billion in the years to come.[23]

Texting is even more convenient and therefore more prevalent than e-mailing. Sometimes I'll be in a different part of the house and text my wife a question. If I spoke loudly, she could hear me, but it's easier to text.

Technology has helped us communicate to the masses, and in no way am I bashing e-mail or texts, but we need to be aware of the trade-off we are making with written-word communication. Look back through history, for instance; wars have been started over a misinterpreted letter from one person to another. Here's a more current example of how easy it is to miscommunicate. I want you to read the following sentence aloud, but each time put the emphasis on the word that's been marked in bold:

I didn't take your parking spot today.
I **didn't** take your parking spot today.
I didn't **take** your parking spot today.
I didn't take **your** parking spot today.
I didn't take your **parking** spot today.
I didn't take your parking **spot** today.
I didn't take your parking spot **today**.

Although you're using the same words, that same sentence can be interpreted in seven different ways. To further complicate things, those of you who were paying attention noticed that there are only seven iterations of the sentence.

---

[23] The Radicati Group, Inc., "Email Statistics Report, 2015-2019," *Radicati. com*, Radicati Group, Inc., http://www.radicati.com/wp/wp-content/uploads/2015/02/Email-Statistics-Report-2015-2019-Executive-Summary.pdf.

We need to be aware of the power our words have and realize the likelihood and range of misinterpretation. It is our responsibility to ensure that the message we're trying to convey to our motivatees comes across clearly. We need to make sure that our impact matches our intent.

The best communicators are great listeners. I'm sure you've heard that before, but it's important to differentiate between listening and hearing. Hearing is merely the reception of sound, whereas listening is an active and intentional effort to glean meaning from what someone is saying. This is a skill, and just like any other it takes time and effort to develop.

One of the critical components of listening is understanding the context in which something is said. As we noticed above, words can have a variety of meanings depending on how they're emphasized. Even words that are stressed in the same way can communicate different things depending on their context.

It can also be challenging to understand the deep emotions someone is trying to communicate if you've never felt them before yourself. I never realized the unique love a parent has for a child until I became a father. No amount of explanation prepared me for that emotion. Even so, we are capable of understanding that there are many things we don't know and being intentionally empathetic to others.

As the motivator, it is my responsibility to make sure I am understood by my motivatee. To do this I need to think of conversations as a tennis match, not a gun fight. A tennis match is fun only if there is someone on the other end sending the ball back, whereas in a gunfight, we do NOT want anyone to return fire.

Communication follows the same basic principles. When I send a thought over to the other side of the court, I expect a specific outcome. If the person receiving the message reacts in a negative way, or a way that surprises me, I must have done a poor job of sending the message (communicating).

Now, some people will not understand you. Maybe their walls are still built too high. If we, as motivators, want to be better at our communication, feel free to ask the motivatee if they understand. Depending on the seriousness of what we are talking about, I might even ask them to repeat back to me what I am saying to make sure we are on the same page.

As motivators, we need to take full blame for others not understanding us. The blame should not be put on them. It is not that they don't understand us; we just didn't communicate well. Proper communication is essential if you want to motivate the unmotivated.

Make it your responsibility to ensure that you are being understood when you speak. But don't slack on your end of the deal in the process; make sure you utterly understand them. It is your choice to be empathetic rather than upset or offended. Decide to respond positively to potentially negative messages. If you don't understand something, ask for clarification—don't just assume.

For the next thirty days, make this an intentional habit. Resolve to listen and not just hear.

CHAPTER 25
THE MYSTERIOUS DAYS
Some Must Have Less Hours

Time is the great equalizer: we all have twenty-four hours in a day!

"I don't have enough time" is a complaint we are all guilty of making. *Inc. Magazine* published an article a few years ago showing how the average employee who worked an 8-hour day was productive only for 2 hours and 53 minutes. That's only 36 percent of their 8-hour day! If that employee was productive 100 percent of the time, they could get a week's worth of work done in less than two days.

We pay employees for their time working. They can take breaks, and in cases of new startups maybe even play a game of ping pong or two. But if they are being paid to work, they should be working. So, if the average employee is only productive 36 percent (or less) of the time, where does the rest of the day go?

According to the article, here is how employees are spending their workday:

- Reading news websites – 1 hour, 5 minutes
- Checking social media – 44 minutes
- Discussing non-work-related things with co-workers – 40 minutes
- Searching for new jobs – 26 minutes
- Taking smoke breaks – 23 minutes

- Making calls to partners/friends – 18 minutes
- Making hot drinks – 17 minutes
- Texting or instant messaging – 14 minutes
- Eating snacks – 8 minutes
- Preparing food in the office – 7 minutes[24]

That doesn't include the amount of time spent in the bathroom. If you have a smartphone, it is like everything has become longer. We waste A LOT of time. Meals take longer now. Not because the discussions are deeper with those you are eating with, but because we are focusing on our phones. I have even found that when employees would 30-45 minute bathroom breaks once smartphones became the norm. The bottom line is we waste more time than we think!

The most commonly heard objection to our LP system is that people don't have the time to do it. Our system literally takes 20 minutes to set up and then 5 minutes at the end of the night. Yet still, people have convinced themselves they don't have enough time. This is like saying, "I am too sick to take the medicine" or "I am too tired to go to sleep!" You are stating the problem with the solution in hand yet choosing not to use it. Unmo tends to do this quite often, so let's make sure we do not become Unmo when it comes to how we spend our time each day.

When we launched our corporate training programs, working with teams of all levels, one of the most interesting responses from a CEO was: "I expected increased productivity and profits. I got those. What I didn't expect was that after bringing Life Pulse in, my team no longer uses the excuse 'I don't have time.'"

---

[24] Betsy Mikel, "You're Really Only Productive for This Many Hours in an 8-Hour Workday, Research Finds," *Inc.com*, October 4, 2017, http://www.inc.com/betsy-mikel/youre-really-only-productive-for-this-many-hours-in-an-8-hour-workday-study-finds.html.

Motivated and unmotivated people all have twenty-four hours in a day. The difference lies in how they choose to use it.

Realize that this excuse usually stems from emotion, not logic. Organization can be useful to combat this: if you show your motivatees how much time they have in their day, that "overwhelmed" feeling tends to dissipate. The LP system is built to do exactly this. If you choose not to use the LP, ask your motivatee to list everything they have to do on a sheet of paper; then organize it. Unmo might not admit it, but doing this quick exercise immediately shows both of you if they are busy and mismanaging their time or just overwhelmed. Overwhelmed can be corrected by logic. Busy can be corrected by helping them delegate. Seeing it on paper allows you, and them, to see what actions need to be taken to resolve the issue. Sometimes the solution is to bring on more help, while other times the solution is for Unmo to work on managing their tasks better so they can do the job you have hired them to do. This exercise takes the emotion out of this decision and uses logic to support what needs to happen next.

In doing this, I have been able to hire when needed or show my team when they need to step up their game and take care of their responsibilities. This has been the simplest way to know if I need to remove things from someone's plate or help them rearrange their tasks in order to show them that they have more room than they think. I am still not sure what is worse: letting someone stay overwhelmed who is overwhelmed or letting someone who feels overwhelmed stay feeling overwhelmed. Both are bad; neither gets you the results you want.

There's a vast difference between *feeling* overwhelmed and *being* overwhelmed. If you can show this to your motivatee, chances are they'll stop using this excuse. Ask yourself and your team these three questions:

1. What do I do from the time I wake up to the time I fall asleep?
2. How much time, if I needed to, could I dedicate to getting what I want done every day?
3. What do I waste my time on?

Make sure your time is not being wasted. Have a plan to use your time effectively, and then teach your motivatee to do the same. Don't be hypocritical: if you're only working 36 percent of the day like the employees in the study, don't ask your motivatee to do more.

THEM - Putting the pieces Together – Post Read

(You + THEM) x System = Results

I am assuming you have read this book from section to section in the order it is written and if you've done this, you have a clearer understanding of how motivation works, you've read and applied the information in the YOU section, and are now in the position to implement the information from the THEM section. Even if you just implemented one of the topics in the THEM section in your relationship with Unmo, you both are in a much better position to succeed than before. If you take all of it and put it into action, you will get a chance to see maximum results for everyone you build a motivational relationship with.

First remember that your expectations are what will help dictate the outcome of what you are working on. When the tyranny of negative expectation creeps into your relationship with Unmo, you are setting yourself and them up for failure. Make sure you remember that motivation is not a character trait but a state of mind. Give the benefit of the doubt to Unmo, not because they deserve it but because the goal is to get a positive result and not a negative result. Do not be naïve but look for the win-win.

Every time you are interacting with Unmo there is an imprint you are leaving. This imprint is either positive or negative but is never neutral. We build motivational walls sometimes without meaning to do it. Make sure when you are interacting with people you are careful with what you say and what you do. Enjoy your time and be yourself. This is a great example of how the YOU portion of the formula. If you work on you properly, you can always be yourself.

We discussed the fact that there is no room for hypocrisy when it comes to motivation. The goal is to spend more time being vs telling. Think about your past experiences. What have you been through that may allow you to better connect with Unmo? Know your story and use it to show how it should be done rather than wasting energy, time, and your breath constantly telling Unmo what should be done.

In life we all have purpose. When someone is in an unmotivated state of mind, it is almost impossible to see their purpose. When following your purpose, it becomes nearly impossible to have this unmotivated mindset. Just because someone is unclear on their purpose does not mean they do not have one. We all do. Many people I have worked with who you would classify as motivated or successful do not know their purpose and they have just been battling through life one step at a time. Once we walk them through our program, there is a relief of clarity that comes over them that explains why they have always done what they have done, how they got where they are today, and even more importantly, how they are going to get where they want to go next. No matter if you are motivated or not – your life has purpose and unlocking it will help you get to the next level of motivation or spark new motivation.

Now that we have discovered purpose, that is like the food to our mind and thoughts that allows us to keep a mindset of motivation. It is as if we will know what it is Unmo wants to eat (what motivates them) and as the motivator, it is our job to properly place what Unmo wants so that Unmo can get it with some work. We do not want to put it out of Unmo's reach because Unmo will quickly get discouraged. The common mistake when setting goals for others (especially Unmo) is the popular saying, "Shoot for the moon because even if you miss, you'll land among the stars." Setting big goals and assuming that will motivate others is a short-term approach that loses its effectiveness immediately when others realize they are not going to achieve the goal. So instead give smaller steps that allow them to succeed. If we know what they want to eat (their purpose) and we know that motivates them, let put the "food bowl" just far enough away where they have to work towards it but the NEED to be able to get it. Once they get it, let them enjoy it for a bit a then you can re position the food bowl. Maybe this time a bit future! The goal is to let Unmo succeed and watch how they become enlightened by this feeling of fulfillment and achievement.

Through this process of Motivate the Unmotivated, communication is the reason why relationships break, and Motivational Walls are created. Communication is difficult. It is taking an emotional thought and uses a logical form to express it. It is exceedingly difficult to do. As the Motivator we need to be the one to recognize when there is a communication breakdown. I do not care if you are as clear as possible, if Unmo is not understanding whatever it is you are saying then you are not saying it in a way that they need to hear it. Take a step back and think about the previous chapters in this book and see where in this system something may have been left out.

No matter how different you are from Unmo we all have 24 hours in a day which we call the great equalizer. No one can make more time however some people get more done than others each day. We all value our time when others waste it, but we seem to excuse it when we waste it. For you and Unmo alike, the issue is not that you don't have time, but it is that we are not prioritizing whatever we say we "want." It is as if we want the end result, but we are not willing to take the actions needed to achieve it. "I do not have time." Is an excuse that will no longer make sense once you connect what we are doing with the System we are about to introduce to you.

In these first two sections of the Motivation Formula, you have managed the 2 variables the best you possibly can. You are in a great position to now put gas on the fire. The safest way to do this is to have proper containment and management of this flame. The system you now choose to use will do one of three things – Grow the flame in a direction you are looking for, grow the flame out of control, or extinguish the flame all together. Time to choose the right system.

KNOWING THE SYSTEM

The universe is full of systems. In fact, it can be argued that the universe exists only *because* of systems. Certain things happen that allow our world to go from the past toward the future. Diving deeper and deeper into the curious world of physics, scientists are discovering that these systems, which have existed since the beginning of time behave like rhythms, discovered over time and can help predict outcomes in the future.

At some point we decided to rebel against systems. It is as if society has told us that structure and systems hold us back. As if structure and systems are too stiff and take our freedom. That could not be future from the truth. This is a dangerous misconception which if exists, came from bad leaders and/or bad systems you have experienced in the past. If you experience a bad leader, there will be so many Motivational Walls build just from the distrust or dislike towards the individual telling to use the system so therefore you did not trust the systems. Without trust in the system or process, understandably you will not give it the attention it needs to be successful.

If you experienced a good leader, you could easily have experienced a bad system. One that was flawed from its foundation. These systems are not sustainable because you suddenly feel like you are putting more effort into the system then results you are experiencing from the system. For a system to work, it takes time and obedience (willingness to follow). Time is needed so you can understand the system and the obedience is so that you follow it properly. Most systems are built like a combination to a safe. If you have all digits but one, you are not getting to whatever is in that safe. All parts are needed to make the system work as planned. The systems we build, and we will discuss, are built differently.

Much easier to use. You will see that they are made up of individual actions that can be done separately and be effective. The beautiful thing about our systems we are about to share is when the individual actions are brought together as they were built to be, you will see exponential return on your efforts.

Before we jump in or jump back in for those who have written off systems, systems are likely uncomfortable to implement. Just think of what we are doing. We are putting a process in our life that forces us to act a way that we would not "normally" act. As humans we do not like change but as humans, we need understand the difference between change and growth: the first is inevitable while the second is intentional. So be ok with it being uncomfortable or challenging in the beginning. It will take time and willingness to follow the system but do not give up because it is challenging. In the past, if you experienced bad leaders or systems, it will be easy for you to give up on a system the second it feels different.

Like we discuss with our clients, let's change our approach when new systems or structures are introduced (as long as it doesn't do irreputable damage.) The best way to figure out if a system works or does not work is to follow it perfectly for the designated time (we usually suggest 10-15 perfectly implemented cycles depending on the system). This means you need to get to the point where you are following the system perfectly and then you do everything you can to prove the system correct for those 10-20 times. The more perfect you are at implementing the system, the faster you can get through this phase. Most of us have become so critical and cynical of anything that is not our own idea that we immediately try to prove things wrong. In our company, we challenge all individuals to do the opposite. Question everything but change your end goal. Instead of living a life where you try to prove things wrong, try to prove things right and you will see an amazing transformation in the results in your life.

The most successful individuals throughout history had their own form of structure and systems throughout their life. They may look different for each person which is why the systems we are introducing can be adapted to any person, any industry, and situation. For example, some individuals work better with one of our coaching programs custom designed for what you need and other just pick up our LP planner and just start cruising along. Recognize, to feel like you are "cruising" through life, individuals need a combination of structure which brings a safe feeling of freedom as well as rhythm which brings a peaceful feeling of progress.

Systems impact us internally by giving us freedom and peace. Although these feelings are internal, they are influenced by the external factors of the system - inputs. Hands down, the most crucial part to the success of any system - the inputs. You have probably heard the phrase "good in equals good out" or "bad in equals bad out." The system we use, the LP, is highly recommended because it will take any honest input, good or bad, and spit out a positive outcome. However, if you lie or hold back, the system will not produce the results that you want. If you follow the guidance of the YOU and THEM sections of this book, getting honest answers for yourself and your motivates will not be challenge but will start to come naturally in conversations.

Although we have a physical planner that we call the LP, the value behind the LP is the resiliency and effectiveness of the system printed on the page. We encourage you to use the LP and get a copy for yourself as well as with Unmo. If Unmo is reluctant use the physical LP, use the nine parts of this system to drive conversation. The 9 questions the LP guides you through are great questions for you to ask them on a daily or weekly basis. Remember to share your own answers as well so that you can connect with them while you are becoming increasingly understanding of what is going on between their two ears.

The LP is built specifically so that as the system is used and you refine your approach, the better the results get. The growth of this system is exponential. With every application, layers are peeled back, always giving you something with which you can work. As with any system, no matter how powerful it may be, getting people on board to use it regularly is one of the hardest things to do. Creating a system is fun and easy but implementing the system consistently and properly is where most people fail.

Of course, you do not have to use this system if you do not wish to, but we could not find anything that could do consistently produce positive results as the LP does. This system is even developed so you can customize it to fit your needs within the separate parts of the system. Again, use the LP or not, that is your decision but no matter what you decide, make sure you are well aware of how the system works before you choose what system to use. By fully understanding the system you select, you will be better equipped to implement that system and, therefore, experience more consistent results.

CHAPTER 26
AN IDEA WITHOUT IMPLEMENTATION IS AS WASTED THOUGHT
The Figure 8 of Implementation

Creating a system to correct a problem is simple; creating a system to prevent a problem is a much larger challenge.

Problems are a part of life and coming up with creative solutions is part of being an adult. When you become a leader, your area of responsibility expands. You're no longer just in charge of creating solutions for your own problems; you have to find answers for other people. This isn't easy, and it often takes quite a bit of work. Thomas Edison is credited for once saying: "There is no elevator to success. You have to take the stairs." If it was Edison who said this, I feel he must have been misquoted. See Edison was known for seeing an issue and creating a solution. Basically, not settling for the status quo but always seeing in terms of how things could be better. It seems throughout his life, anytime there was "no elevator" he created one. He is known for his successful and creative solutions, inventions, and systems. How can we be like him in this sense?

It is rare to have a problem that consists exclusively of an immediate or a long-term need. I see people focusing on one and excluding the other far too often. Here's an example: you're in the middle of a lake when your boat springs a leak. There are multiple problems, but here are two major problems and two potential solutions:

Problem 1 - Water is coming into the boat.
Problem 2 - Water is in the boat.

Solution 1 - Stop the water from coming into the boat.
Solution 2 - Get the water out of the boat.

Which do you take care of first? The answer to this problem is the same as it is for 90 percent of business questions: it depends. First, we need to evaluate the nature of the problem. If the hole is a small one and you have a big bucket, you might want to bail the water out first. If the leak is a significant one and water is coming in faster than you can get rid of it, maybe the hole should be plugged first.

When your motivatee encounters an obstacle, it could be an immediate issue or a long-term dilemma—more likely, it's both. Throwing out a suggestion for a long-term solution might not be the most appropriate thing to do at the moment. Sometimes, it's better to help them address the immediate concern, bring the chaos level down to a calm state, then have a follow-up conversation about how to prevent this from recurring in the future.

There are two parts to this lesson. The first is learning how to separate the two issues, and the second is implementing the system.

The easiest way to start is to get a piece of paper or a whiteboard and write out your thoughts. What is happening? What are the core issues at play? Who are the players, and what are their roles? When we try to solve something in our head, it's like trying to solve a puzzle without taking it out of the box. It's astounding how much clarity will immediately come to the solution when you get it out in writing. This allows you to work through the dilemma, understanding the immediate need and the long-term, underlying issue.

We need to make the jump from problem to solution, but we need to do it in a way that makes most sense to the current situation. The goal is discovering a problem and then find a solution. Dwelling on the problem once it is recognized and understood (there is water in the boat), is detrimental to any progress towards a solution and now our focus (getting the water out of the boat.)

If we pay too much attention to the immediate need (e.g., get the water out of the boat)), we might spend years bailing water. If we focus exclusively on the long-term (e.g., patching the hole so water won't come in), the boat might sink from the weight of the water filling up inside. Both sides of the issue often need to be worked on simultaneously, but the priority you assign is dependent on the situation. When there is a problem, we want solutions immediately and before there is a problem, we want solutions to prevent the problem. They best way to avoid a problem is through a systematic approach that has predictable outcomes. No matter if it is a short-term or long-term solution, preventative or reactive, when you implement a new system, the most important thing to do is to maintain consistency. If you don't do this, the system quickly becomes irrelevant. With life being so unpredictable, stability is the best way to handle the unknown.

The goal of a system is for this step by step process to bring from the beginning to the end. Although it is rarely his smooth, it looks like the straight line below. In order to get a system to go from the beginning to the end, think of your systems as a circle vs a straight line. Even if the final step of your system is to start over again, as long as the system starts over, it can now be duplicated. As we bring these systems to others, we now need to remember that there are two parties to any act of motivation. Even if you are introducing this new system to someone else or a group of people, we now need the second circle to represent them.

I want you to recognize this illustration of two circles coming together. As you can imagine, there is a system to implementing systems. All you need to do is take those two circles for you and them and stack them for you to see the Figure 8 of Implementation. Most people have introduced a system and that is a pretty simple task. One step... tell someone about it. For most people, the goal of introducing a system is for the system to be implemented but just introducing it is RARELY enough. There needs to be buy in from those who are introduced to it. By Following the Figure 8 of Implementation, you will easily be able to introduce ideas in a way that can be simply implemented by yourself and others. An idea without implementation is a wasted thought!

> ## An idea without implementation is a wasted thought!

They may seem more pertinent to business settings; however, they will work for personal and family relationships as well. Better yet, these same eight steps aren't just there to hold multiple people; they can help you implement a system in your own life as well.

Step 1 - EXPLANATION WORKSHOP/WALK-THROUGH

This first step is essential. Walk every affected person through the system, focusing not only on how it works, but why it works. Depending on what you are trying to implement, it can be as simple as a walk-through over the phone, or it can be a more complex, full-day training workshop. If your employees don't understand the system, it will never be as effective or self-implemented as it could be.

Here is where a lot of people go wrong. They shoot out an e-mail with a slide show and assume that everything will immediately work flawlessly. Set your team up for success by giving them the adequate training and the tools they need to succeed. Don't rush this. Make the investment in doing it right from the beginning; you will save time and resources on the backend. If you are the leader, you should ONLY do this workshop or walkthrough if you are using this system as part of your life or role. If it is just a new system that you learned recently, one that you are still trying to figure out, do not just throw it on your team. Take time to be able to teach from experience with what the system has done for your life before introducing it. Most of the times, the best approach is to bring in a third party to conduct a training session.

LinkedIn and Study.com co-sponsored a study in 2017 that examined how much businesses were investing in their employees.[25] The average organization spent $1,273 per employee over the course of a year, while small organizations with fewer than 500 workers invested an average of $2,016 per employee. Where does your business fall in this area?

Step 2 - WEEKLY REMINDERS

Some managers believe that their teams don't need reminders, and I think this is crazy. If a team is perfect and never needs to be prompted, they don't need a manager...and therefore they do not need you! A leader's goal shouldn't be to "catch" their subordinates using or not using a system. Instead, it should be to guide them as they learn, directing their efforts so the system has the best chance of success.

---

[25] https://www.td.org/soir2018? If so, it looks like it was co-sponsored by LinkedIn and American Management Association International.

When you implement a new system, you should be reminding your team on a weekly basis to use it. The most effective way to remind your team of the system is being vs telling. As the leader, you want to be a walking example of what is expect and to use the system. As a secondary reminder, which is one most people mistakenly rely on, is to remind them through telling. Both work and when combined work even better but do not undervalue how helpful a simple reminder can be when done well. Remember that encouragement removes the need for enforcement, when done properly. Make sure they're not reverting to their old habits. Even once the system has been established, we found weekly reminders are desired by both manager and employees.

Reminders shouldn't consist of a weekly nagging e-mail but should contain a helpful tip, related articles, or an interesting video to watch. We send out what we call "Weekly Wisdom" e-mails to all of our users and teams. We found it gives them a great way to start off their week, reminding them to plan their week while also keeping them engaged with new and relevant content to their work and life.

Step 3 - WEEKLY CHECK-INS

Reminders are one-way and merely serve as a prompt. Check-ins are fundamentally different and should involve two-way communication. Use this meeting as a thermometer to gauge the temperature of the team. Ask questions! Are there any issues that you can help resolve? Even a question as simple as, "What are the top three things you're accomplishing this week?" will give you great insight into what is happening with your motivatees.

Be careful of how you use these meetings. If they become negative in nature, you'll quickly destroy any willingness on your team's part to engage with you authentically. The overarching theme of every interaction from your end should be summarized by the question: "How can I help you succeed?"

I always encourage face-to-face meetings but do whatever is necessary to make this happen consistently. Even a text or e-mail is better than nothing.

Step 4 - DAILY USE OF THE SYSTEM

Not all systems are designed to be used daily. If that's the case, modify this bullet to reflect the shortest period of time it should be used, whether that's hourly, daily, weekly, monthly, or quarterly. The point is to make sure that it's consistent.

As you can probably predict, the most important person to be seen using whatever you are implementing is you. Make sure you are not just acting like you are using it but truly using it in your life. This is something that needs to be real as if you pretend to be using it, you will be found out quickly. It is difficult for others to stay consistent with new programs and systems so make sure you recognize this. Make sure you feel the struggles that you are putting others through. Make sure you can relate and express to them that you understand how difficult it is, but you also can share the benefits you are experiencing through all of this.

Step 5 - PHYSICAL REPRESENTATION (NOT DIGITAL)

The more of our five senses that we can incorporate into a system, the easier it is to build a habit. Having a physical representation, as a reminder of the system, is very beneficial. This could be a poster, a mascot, or a physical book. Taking the system out of the digital realm and putting it into the physical world increases the likelihood of success.

It's easy to send out e-mails, but the average open rate of an e-mail in the business world is less than 40 percent. Nearly two-thirds of e-mails are never opened. Sending a personal letter, however, increases the chance that a message will be received. This is why we took our LP system and put it on paper, bound it, and created the LP Planner. It is now a physical thing that individuals can experience through their senses. Each time the see it or touch it, they are reminded by the systems we are teach. . It represents productivity in our clients' offices, and it's easy to check if someone has their "blues" with them when they're needed.

Just the site of the physical representation, in this case the LP planner, is enough to remind individuals of what they should be doing. They may not jump on board right away but the more they are exposed to the system through physical representations, the harder it is for them to avoid. With proper time and consistent exposure, people will start using the systems you want to implement.

Step 6 - UNIVERSAL USE (ALL-IN COMMITMENT)

Systems need to be used at every level from the top down. Some systems are specific to a certain role so when I say "used at every level" it means that whoever is jumping in for that role, no matter what position they have at the company, follows whatever systems should be done for that role.

In the example of our LP it is simple. Everyone from the leader down should be using it in everyday life. For other systems, it may be based on a specific position. Even if it a system on how a bathroom should be cleaned by your team, it doesn't matter if it is the janitor who is doing it or the CEO, the system should be followed every time properly. It does not matter who is taking the actions. When a system is universally used, the output is consistent because the inputs do not change.

The biggest abusers we see when implementing systems are people at the top expecting everyone else to follow the system while they think they have a better way of doing it. The motivator , the motivatee and everyone in between needs to use what systems you want implemented. If you implement a system in pieces, the best you can hope for is fragmented results.

Step 7 - QUARTERLY REVIEW/REFINE

A review is different from a check-in. Think of check-ins as the dashboard gauges in your car. They give an indication of the immediate actions in which your vehicle is engaged. Reviews are more like a safety inspection, where the vehicle is put on a lift and a number of things under the hood are inspected to ensure everything is running as it should be.

How often your system is used will determine how frequently you need to review it. I recommend never going more than a quarter without a systematic evaluation. But unless you see harmful issues or blatant problems, give the system the time it needs before you start changing it. Please remember, this is about implementing a system that is already shown to work. This is not part of building a system. When reviewing a system that is already shown to work, the goal is to not change the system but to change the inputs. Changing your actions or the path you are traveling may be necessary but there is no way of knowing this until you are using the system properly and regularly.

I like to call this the "Review/Refine" process because if you find a problem, you should fix it. This doesn't mean that your system has failed or you're admitting defeat; it merely means you encountered an obstacle and can create a solution. You can adjust how a system works without changing the system itself.

If during this Review and Refine process, your actions are perfect and constant, this is what I call a plateau. This is the time I would review the system and see if it is working the way you want it too. It is EXCEEDINGLY rare, for a system that works, to need to be changed. It is QUITE common for the specific actions or the specific implementation of that system needs to be changed as it is being introduced to new groups and as the environment changes.

This Review and Refine process allows you to do more of what is working and less of what isn't working. Focus on adapting TO the change leaves you behind. Focus on adapting WITH change gives you momentum. Adapt with the changes of the world through changing your actions rather than changing your systems

Step 8 - UNDERSTAND THE WHY

When you ask your team to do something different, you need to understand what you're asking at its very core, philosophical level. Why is this happening? Why is it important? And why is it necessary? If you can't answer those questions immediately—and enthusiastically—the chances of convincing your team will substantially decrease. We can't assume that people will just follow us blindly, and we need to be comfortable with lots of Q&A-type interaction. This is where an external facilitator can be helpful.

Don't skip any steps when you introduce a new system. If you're asking your team to change the way they operate, make sure you have good reasons. Every time you implement a new system, review this checklist and make sure you follow the Figure 8 of Implementation and have all eight steps in place to make your stools study enough for multiple people to stand on.

- ☐ Explanation Workshop/Walk-Through
- ☐ Weekly Reminders
- ☐ Weekly Check-Ins
- ☐ Daily Use of System
- ☐ Physical Representation
- ☐ Universal Use (All-In)
- ☐ Quarterly Review
- ☐ Understand the Why

CHAPTER 27
WHY DON'T WE PLAN?
Lessons from Mike Tyson

The plan itself means nothing. Planning means everything.

A plan is merely the end result of the planning process. Thinking through a series of potential outcomes, understanding the resources and position you have, and then creating a plan of action instills in you a sense of confidence, excitement, and peace. Even if you never end up using that particular plan, you're much better off for having gone through the process.

A mentor of mine is one of the top trainers for Navy SEALs. One time he was explaining that SEALs hate surprises, so they plan for every possible outcome. Sometimes they'll spend months or even years training for a mission that takes minutes. Although the vast majority of their contingency plans go unused, the process of planning allows each member of the team to become so comfortable with their teammates and the overall approach that they function as a single, organic unit. Rank structure often goes out the window, and whoever is best suited for a particular task seamlessly takes charge. There is little to no discussion. There is little to no time to think. And there is little to no time to debate anyone's decision. Some SEALs even have trouble explaining how it works when this is done correctly, but a number have said it is as if they know what everyone else is thinking without any traditional communication.

Could you imagine that being you and the people in your life? How about even a fraction of that ability to work as one? Imagine how much planning and practice it would take to get your co-workers, or family, to operate that well together.

The time for discussion, debate, and disagreement is during the planning part. That is when we can throw out ideas we do not like or have our "two cents" heard. During the execution of the plan itself, each part of the "unit" should be busy doing their part. At this point, there will be no time for discussion, debate, or disagreement.

Besides being a champion boxer, Mike Tyson is known for producing some pretty outlandish quotes. During one interview, a reporter outlined the detailed strategy his opponent was preparing for an upcoming fight. Tyson shrugged and replied in only a way that he could: "Everyone has a plan until they get punched in the face."

Life throws punches at us all the time. As crazy as it might sound, these punches, when handled properly, are what allow us to grow and feel fulfilled. Conversely, when we are not ready for the punches, the smallest jab can feel like a knock-out.

We commonly refer to our 80/20 principle of planning: 80 percent of the things that happen in life can be planned for, while 20 percent cannot. However, if we do not manage the 80 percent we can plan, the 20 percent for which we cannot plan can feel like 100 percent of our life. This is when we become overwhelmed, and sometimes paralyzed, by our perception of reality. Sometimes we focus so much on the 20 percent that we ignore the things we can prepare for, despite them being four times more common than the unexpected!

We all can create excuses as to why we do not plan. Maybe in the past, planning has not worked out as expected. Or maybe we feel that we do not have time. These reasons are counterintuitive. If you do not have time, or you have had issues achieving the desired outcome in the past, then you *need* to plan.

For nearly a decade, I lived in Atlanta, Georgia, where the traffic makes no sense. Like many cities, there is no telling what traffic will be like during a Saturday afternoon. The traffic is always unpredictable—and rarely in a way that's in your favor.

What amazes me is when people use this as an excuse. This is something we all know exists, yet we feel justified to walk into a meeting ten minutes late and say, "Sorry, traffic was bad."

We need to make sure we stop doing that. If you have kids, you know that it will take you longer to pack for a quick trip to the park with them than it used to take you to pack for two-week vacations without kids. If you are working with a client or vendor who is always a bit behind on their deadlines, then we need to have that in our plan.

Planning for these things will not help you avoid them, but it will help you avoid a problem. When it comes to planning, the reason why we tend to get derailed so quickly is because we forget to add in a margin for the time it may take. I have no problem sitting in traffic if I am not late. If I leave my house fifteen minutes late and then all of a sudden, I am fifteen minutes late for a meeting because traffic is a bit worse than I thought, that is when I catch myself critiquing every driver and how their lack of skill in driving is what is causing me to be late.

We need to think as the SEALs do during the planning process and realize that the plan itself means nothing, but planning means everything. When you are planning, think of two to three things that could throw you off your plan. Then determine what you need to do to create that margin so that you are not completely derailed if it happens. I always like to add an extra 10 to 20 percent more time to a task than I think it needs to make sure it receives the attention it deserves. I have never been stressed out for getting to an event or meeting too early. I always can find something to do during these few moments of downtime.

Creating a margin is what makes planning extremely worthwhile. Avoid scheduling every little increment of time available throughout the day. You will quickly find that if you do not schedule a margin in your day, you will fail at your plan, which will begin to lose value. To Mike Tyson's point, everyone has a plan until they get punched in the face, but there are people whom Tyson did punch in the face who were able to take it and beat him. Getting punched in the face is more detrimental when you do not know it is coming. Life is going to throw punches at you, so don't let them surprise you. Instead, anticipate it, plan for it, and then come back with a counter that makes that punch seem like it never happened.

Spend ten to twenty minutes planning your week. This small investment will provide huge returns in your ability to manage everything that life throws your way. Work with your schedule and your motivatee to add 10 to 20 percent extra time to tasks that deserve it; that way, you and your motivatee are not rushed. Focus on the planning part of the process, and make sure you are thinking of what could throw you or your motivatee off. Allow communication to happen so that when you get the opportunity to execute the plan, few things will be able to drastically throw you off your path.

CHAPTER 28
USING THE LP AS A MOTIVATEE
Get More Done for You

Failing to plan is planning to fail.

The common basis of decision-making, for almost every life form on earth, revolves around one central principle: What will help them live longer? Think about trees. You probably learned in school that the way you determine the age of a tree is by counting the number of rings in its trunk. What you might not know is that those rings appear when under an immense amount of stress.

These same forces happen in our lives. A good friend of mine, Dr. Austin Cohen, uses the term "Expansion Cycles." These are times in our life that are hard. We're struggling, we're going through a lot of stress, but it's during these times that we could experience the most growth.

Trees try to grow as high as they can because they know that the higher, they get, the more likely they are to receive the sunlight necessary for life. Branches aren't just for decoration. They're intentional offshoots that the plant uses to send leaves to an area where the sun is shining. Growing branches and leaves is stressful for the tree and takes a lot out of it, but these are tangible examples of growth. In the winter, the tree sheds its leaves and rests. The tree faithfully follows these work and rest cycles every year until it dies.

Humans aren't as consistent. When we get out of our rhythm or routine, we become less effective, and our intentional growth slows tremendously. Some people avoid routines on purpose, thinking that it will inhibit their freedom. What they don't realize is that when they refuse to take part in intentionally creating a rhythm, that doesn't mean it doesn't happen. It just gets built without them. We all live in some kind of routine. The difference between successful and unsuccessful people is often the part they play in shaping that.

Having a routine doesn't mean you become a workaholic. Rest is just as important as work, and having the right balance gives you the best chance at growth. Sometimes it's the right call to binge-watch Netflix for eight hours—just make sure it is an intentional call. My father recently retired from a phenomenally successful career as a dentist. He built a substantial practice over several decades, raised four kids, maintained a happy marriage, and was active in the community. This all took a tremendous amount of hard work. He was watching me speak one time, and when the moment for audience participation came, he asked for the mic. I'll admit, I was a little nervous. Even though I speak professionally, having one of my parents in the audience, now with a mic, is far from typical. He turned around, looked at the audience, and said: "I've known about the LP system for a while. I'm retired now so you might think I'm done with systems. That isn't true. Systems are just as important now as at any point in my life. I have found when you have the freedom to do nothing, it's really easy to just do nothing."

That's a profound statement. Rest has a purpose and is absolutely necessary. When we don't have a system in place, though, rest ceases to be deliberate and becomes our default. Then we stop growing.

Living a balanced and enjoyable life involves mimicking nature's growth patterns. We have to stay in a rhythm and use a system that allows you to do this. This is where the LP system comes into play. It was designed with nature in mind and takes only a small investment of twenty minutes at the beginning of the week and five minutes each night to map out the next day.

As you go through the following nine questions, write out your answers. If it is easy for you, or your motivatee, to answer all nine questions quickly and accurately, then you have an amazing and unusual grasp on your life. If it takes you time to really get to the heart of these, like most people, you will be amazed at the results just by answering these questions before you or your motivatees start the week. Maria and I do this every week, then share our answers with each other. I would challenge you to do the same with the ones you are trying to motivate or build a relationship with.

1. **One-Word Focus:** What's the one word you should focus on to accomplish what you need to get done this week?
2. **Quote:** What's a quote will define what you mean by your one-word focus?
3. **Gratitude:** What are you grateful for?
4. **Weekly Wisdom:** What did you learn last week that you can implement this week?
   a. Message us through our website or social media, and I will personally send you one each week for free.
5. **Pulse Check:** How well have you balanced your time/life in the Four Vital Signs of Fulfillment (Internal/Relational/Physical/Professional)?
6. **Goals:** What do you want to accomplish this week in the Four Vital Signs of Fulfillment?
7. **Brain Dump:** What do you logistically need to do this week?

8. **Event Manager:** What are your top priorities based on your goals and urgency?
9. **Daily Schedule:** What events do you have scheduled or need to schedule?

This is the basic structure for the LP system a system, and it will allow you to see what you need to accomplish clearly. I use the LP when I'm at work as well as on vacation. Staying within the system allows me to be more productive when I'm working and more relaxed when I'm not.

Most people live like they're trying to put together the puzzle of life without even taking it out of the box. That invites a lot of frustration. The best way to solve a puzzle is to dump it out on a large area where you can see the big picture, then search for the outside pieces so you can build a framework. Once this is complete, finishing the puzzle becomes simple and rewarding.

That's what the LP system does. It allows you and your motivatee to brain dump and get everything out where you can see it. Then you can create a structure that puts everything else in your life in the proper place. Once that's done, going through the motions, just like finishing a puzzle, becomes a simple task.

Try this for the next four weeks. Make sure you, as a motivator, do this. Take the time to understand the LP system. You can do it with your motivatee at the same time if you want, but the key here is for you to use it yourself. If you want, we have physical LPs that you can order from our website to help guide you and your motivatee through the process. But using those nine questions every week will add to the structure of your life significantly, even without the physical LP

CHAPTER 29
USING THE LP AS A MOTIVATOR
Get More Done for Them

Don't serve a dish you wouldn't eat yourself.

When I think of the word "busy," I picture a crowded place with thousands of people moving through it. The best representation of this scene is the Atlanta airport, which moves over 100 million passengers every year, making it the busiest airport in the world. I decided this was the perfect place to use as a litmus test to confirm the strength our LP system: if it worked here, it would work anywhere.

I was able to get a meeting with the CEO of Atlanta Airlines Terminal Corporation (AATC), Kofi Smith. He agreed to bring me in and teach his team how to use the system. Although we received the highest exit survey score AATC had ever recorded for a third-party instructor, there were a select few attendees who did not fully implement the system initially. They had the blue books but were not maximizing the system. In the beginning, Kofi, being as busy as he is, was one of those who didn't fully engage, even though he had brought me in.

At this time in his life, he was not only responsible for safely moving 100 million plus people each, managing thousands of employees, and being a good husband and father, but he was also pursuing his doctorate as well. He did what many of us do when we're completely overloaded: he saw a tool that could help him, but he didn't have the mental energy to invest in implementing it.

However, Kofi reached a breaking point. He was overloaded. He knew something had to change, so he opened his LP and gave it a chance. The system worked and allowed him to manage his myriad of responsibilities while completing his PhD; he now goes by Dr. Kofi Smith.

As Dr. Smith implemented the system in his life, he began advocating it to his subordinates. We're able to track usage rates among our clients through e-mail open rates and the number of views our Weekly Wisdom e-mails receive. We noticed a massive uptick of users from AATC after Kofi began personally using the system.

Real leaders lead by example, and Dr. Smith is one of the strongest leaders I have ever met. Because they trusted him, they did what he did. He not only talked the talk, but he also walked the walk—and they followed.

If you don't like brussels sprouts, don't serve them to your guests. We should never advocate for a system that we're not using ourselves. Earlier in the book, we covered how there is no room in motivation for hypocrisy, and that's just as critical when implementing a system.

I use this system myself and go through it with every employee, co-worker, and client I have. I even use it in my marriage. Maria and I complete our LP and go through them together every Sunday night in a session called "Pulse Check." It takes about ten minutes and is very informal. I was amazed at how much I was missing before we started this. She's the most important person in my life, and I love everything about her. Even though I am with her every single day, I felt like I didn't really get to understand deeply all that goes on in her life until we started sharing these moments on a weekly basis. It was very eye-opening. Once you begin doing this consistently with someone, it's nearly impossible not to know how to motivate them.

Remember, too, that these answers are their answers, and you might disagree with them. As good motivators, we can help guide them to redirect their focus but not change it just to satisfy us. The motivatee needs to feel safe to express their answers and never have an answer shot down, just redirected. As you continue to do this, the refining process tends to naturally happen, as long as the motivator does not belittle any answer given. The goal of using this system as a motivator is to better understand where the motivatee is at in the current week. Be supportive and help direct them but allow the motivatee to discover the roadblocks and missed opportunities for themselves.

Here is what we ask and what we can expect from each answer:

One-Word Focus

- *What you ask*: "What's the one word you should focus on to accomplish what you need to get done this week?"
- *What you get*: Once you know what's on someone's mind, it's much easier to lead them. If your focus for them is A and their focus is on B, neither of you will be satisfied with the week's results.

Gratitude

- *What you ask*: "What is one thing you are grateful for this week?"
- *What you get*: This question gives you insight into each person's motivation. A typical management mistake is to use motivators

that would drive ourselves forward, rather than customizing those solutions to fit what others want.

Weekly Wisdom

- *What you ask:* Before you ask, you can use our system or create custom pieces of wisdom to send to your team. Then ask, "What are your thoughts on the Weekly Wisdom? What does it mean to you?"
- *What you get:* Sharing bits of weekly wisdom with your team is an excellent way to slowly and steadily shape the culture in the way you want. Hearing what their thoughts are about it shows you how aligned your team is with where you want them to be.

Pulse Check

- *What you ask:* "How well did you do in living the week you planned?"
- *What you get:* Not only do you gain insight into how well each member of your team did, but you give them the opportunity to self-evaluate and self-correct. This makes everyone's job easier and less frustrating.

Weekly Goals

- *What you ask:* "What goals do you have in and out of work this week?"
- *What you get:* A good manager knows his team's goals. A good leader understands the individual goals of everyone who is on the team. If you know what someone is trying to achieve outside of work, you can help align their job with those goals, creating a win-win.

Brain Dump

- *What you ask*: "What do you have going on this week?"
- *What you get*: We all have blind spots and hearing an unfiltered perspective on what your motivatees think you're directing them to do is invaluable. A regular check-in like this gives you the opportunity to clarify, course correct, and keep everyone on the same page. If they're missing any task that needs to get done, this is an excellent opportunity to remind them.

Event Manager

- *What you ask*: "What tasks are urgent, and goal related, for you to complete this week?"
- *What you get*: Priorities are subjective even when you, the motivator, set them. Hearing how your team prioritizes their workload will allow you to accurately guide them and move the entire organization toward the goal more efficiently.

Daily Schedule

- *What you ask*: "What does your week look like? What events are already scheduled in your week?"
- *What you get*: You want your employees to work offensively, not defensively. Reminding them to plan their workday and week regularly transforms the entire nature of their job.

Commit to trying this system for four weeks with whomever is important in your life. It could be your spouse, your team at work, or a direct subordinate who needs a little extra attention. Implement the system in your own life first; then introduce it to the other person. It's also helpful to have a copy of the LP for each person so that they can have time to think about the questions on their own and then bring their answers to discuss with you at another time.

CHAPTER 30
BARE-ASS MINIMUM
Get it, Got it, Give me Some More

Know what we need to get, and then give once we get it.

I needed to motivate the employees in one of my companies. The company was doing well, and several members of the team had asked for a bigger piece of the pie, as far as profits were concerned. My initial response was to ask them if they were willing to share in the loss if we had a down quarter. That caused them to sit back and think about their original request. Everyone wants to be an owner when the company is profitable, but that desire disappears when things go downhill.

However, I wanted to reward my employees. I asked a mentor (Steven J. Anderson - (Founder of Total Patients Services Institute & Co-Founder of Crown Council) for advice on the situation. How could I determine a fair way to give them a greater percentage of the profits? His first question was to ask me what my B.A.M. was. I hadn't heard this term before, so I asked him to define it. "B.A.M. stands for Bare-Ass Minimum, and it's the minimum profit margin you need for the company to be successful."

When it comes to business, if you ask someone how much of a margin they would like to see in profit, they would say, "As much as possible." We can have large and ambitious goals; however, we want to make sure that we are realistic with the others with whom we work. In other words, expecting perfection out of everyone you work with is even more unfair than expecting perfection out of yourself. That is why I use the concept of B.A.M. With B.A.M., I was able to explain the exact profit margins I expected from each part of our company. Once we hit that number, we could offer bonuses to those involved. B.A.M. was based only on what was coming in and out of that part of the company.

I crunched a bunch of numbers and decided that the B.A.M. for this company was 20 percent. I called the employees together and explained that once we went over 20 percent profit, they would get a bonus that would be split equally among the team members. The most amazing part was we added a bonus in there that our team (full of individuals who had Connectivity and Support as their Motivation Catalysts) can donate the companies money on their own behalf, to a local organization they felt connected too. This would only happen if we hit the BAM goal.

They immediately got excited and started working hard not only to increase sales but to decrease expenses as well. They took more ownership and responsibility in the company, knowing that if we hired another person, their share of the profit pool would decrease. I essentially had turned them all into company owners without giving up equity or them taking any true liability. The amazing part was that any time we did not hit it, they were more let down that they couldn't give money away. When we did hit it, they enjoyed the money, but sometimes individuals would give their bonus to the cause we donated to. It is all about tapping into what it is they value and how can we connect the dots for them in their work every day.

One of my favorite sayings is "Pigs get fat; hogs get slaughtered." This means that you, as the leader, need to know when enough is enough. If you set your B.A.M. correctly, it gives you a benchmark where you know everything over B.A.M. is gravy. I accepted that I would make 20 percent and everything above that, I'd give back. As a result, our sales increased. That 20 percent became larger, while I was simultaneously able to provide some fantastic benefits to my team.

This principle can be applied in any setting that involves effort and reward, from a company to a family to a nonprofit community group. Select the goal you want to meet, and then be okay with that being enough and gift those who have helped you reach what you needed.

Find your B.A.M. for every area in your life that truly matters. Set realistic expectations for yourself and others and commit to rewarding extraordinary effort. Remember, 80 percent done by someone else is sometimes better than 100 percent done by yourself. The goal in motivating others is not perfection, but progress.

> *The goal in motivating others is not perfection, but progress.*

CHAPTER 31
IT'S OKAY TO WANT THE IMPOSSIBLE
Deadlines Bring Ideas to Life

No sane person would ever run a race without a finish line.

Elon Musk, the billionaire CEO of Tesla and SpaceX, is known for attempting and achieving the impossible. The way he gets these kinds of results is simple. He doesn't just ask his team to do something; he asks them to take ownership of it. One SpaceX engineer told Musk's biographer: "He doesn't say, 'You have to do this by Friday at 2 pm.' He says, 'I need the impossible done by Friday at 2 pm. Can you do it?'"[26]

He doesn't sugarcoat things. He acknowledges that it's difficult, even impossible, and then asks for it anyway. He asks for buy-in from the people actually working on the project, and they commit of their own volition. Setting that finish line for yourself is both scary and exciting at the same time, creating motivation that drives you toward the result.

Another influential leader was Steve Jobs. This man was the definition of a visionary, creating products we didn't know we needed until we held them in our hands. Although I don't agree with every aspect of Jobs' leadership style, one thing that I find incredible is

---

[26] Jenna Goudreau, "Elon Musk and Steve Jobs' Brilliant Trick to Inspire Employees to Achieve the Impossible," CNBC.com, last updated April 20, 2017, http://www.cnbc.com/2017/04/20/elon-musk-steve-jobs-management-trick-to-inspire-employees.html.

what an Apple employee termed his "reality distortion field." The phrase described his charisma and the effects it had on the team with whom he was working.

Employees described the effects like this:

> "In his presence, reality is malleable. He can convince anyone of practically anything."

> "It enabled Jobs to inspire his team to change the course of computer history with a fraction of the resources of Xerox or IBM. It was a self-fulfilling distortion. You did the impossible because you didn't realize it was impossible."[27]

Both Musk and Jobs pushed their teams to limits they never knew they could reach and gave them strict deadlines that needed to be met. Timelines and deadlines are critical in getting things done. Without these, we can languish forever in pursuit of a goal without ever accomplishing it.

Breaking large goals down into smaller chunks that are easier to handle is important. Set deadlines according to these smaller tasks; then use these pieces to build the overall structure of what you're trying to accomplish. Offer rewards for completing these milestones: "$50 for whoever makes the most calls today" or "I'll take you lunch if you finish this task by noon." The rewards don't have to be big, but if you do this consistently enough, you'll start to see results.

They do, however, need to be time oriented. Daily, weekly, or monthly is fine; perhaps even quarterly if the task requires it. The

---

[27] Ibid.

danger here is putting rewards so far out that they seem out of reach, causing employees to lose their motivational capacity.

When my daughter Natalie, or Nat G as we call her, was at the age where she should be learning to crawl I noticed something that all humans experience. Granted my daughter has a rare version of muscular dystrophy but we did not know this information until later in life. Instead of crawling, she would kind of get on her belly and squirm or roll towards where she wanted to go. As I watched her, I found that she has her own motivational boundaries of things that are too far away for her to care about. If a toy she wants is within three feet, she'll overcome any obstacle to get to it. If it's beyond three feet, however, she has no interest. It's as if the toy is a lost cause.

As we have come to find about Natalie's condition (a rare form of muscular dystrophy called MFM8), we are recognizing that she will battle this disease her whole life. What we are trying to do with her is literally impossible according to modern day science. It is not something that just goes away. Because of this, I need to be INCREDIBLY careful as to how I motivate her. She has a whole different set of motivational boundaries that I need to respect. Every day we try to work on crawling, standing, and walking. I want to keep motivation at a high while keeping discouragement at a low.

In the beginning of this book I told you the story of me being the hardest person I ever had to motivate. I am sitting down at our kitchen table, while Natalie is watching cartoons on the chair in front of me. She turns to Maria and asks her, "Can your husband stay with me while you go get my brother." She turns around to me and sends me a big smile. This is my newest, most rewarding, and most challenging motivational relationship I have.

My motivatee (Nat) is such an amazing and motivated little girl. She is the THEM part of the formula that I need to fully understand by helping her realize her PVTT for each exercise we do no matter how little she wants to do it. The easiest way for me to do this is to recognize her motivational catalysts with her motivational boundaries. The YOU variable of the motivational relationship, me, is a challenging one. There is no logical reason to think I can help change this and in fact there is a better chance that my actions, if not under control, could be detrimental to this relationship. I need to bring the best version of me to this relationship.

Once I have those two (YOU and THEM part of the motivational formula), I need to follow the system that is given to us by our support team of doctors and experts. This is the only way we could ever overcome what has been told to us to be impossible and achieve the results that we want so badly.

In the situation with Natalie, if she ever walks, whenever it happens, we would be ecstatic. However, when we are doing tasks, we need to have an end point. If I was to have her try to stand until she fails, it would be a loss every time we work. Instead we ALWAYS have a set amount we are going to do, and I help her as little as I can to achieve those goals.

Motivatees in a professional setting need these same finish lines. You need to place deadlines and rewards far enough away so that they are challenged but close enough that they're achievable. Break quarterly goals into monthly objectives and monthly objectives into weekly tasks.

A great example is with one of our clients we coach from Twitter. It doesn't matter if you are an individual or team that we are coaching but when you are part of our higher-level consulting/coaching program, we set goals this exact way. When we were working with this particular client, we had trouble because they felt some of the goals, they wanted to achieve were just not possible. When we discussed the goal in its entirety, it seemed too big. It seemed overwhelming and just too far out of reach. When we broke down their customized plan, started seeing simple weekly steps they could take. This task all of a sudden seems manageable and became very possible. Not only did it seem manageable, but when they started working towards the goal, the arrived at the goal that was thought of as impossible, much faster than they expected.

Set short-term goals for you and your motivatees that lead to more significant accomplishments. Make deadlines challenging but achievable. Help your motivatee break down big goals into smaller, more manageable steps with finite deadlines that need to be met. Again, the goal is to make these achievable. By doing this, you and your motivatee will quickly realize that success is just the sum of all the little actions you have taken.

SYSTEM - Putting the Pieces Together – Post Read

(You + Them) x SYSTEM = Results

This is where it gets fun. The System is a multiplier to the motivational relationship between the motivator and the motivatee. Depending on the effectiveness and proper implementation of this system, the multiplier can be massive. Planning how you will implement is simple but do not under value the process of selecting the right system. The system is especially important and once you choose the system that you are confident will work, it is now time to change ALL of your focus on follow through. See systems work on their own, we just need to make sure we are following through with what is needed to keep the system working!

The first two sections were more or less actions you as the motivator need to take in order to discover what is needed to motivate the motivatee. This section is not about discovering but is more about following through. Systems are not difficult to create. In fact, we are suggesting not to waste your time creating a system. There are so many out there that work well, so to start this process use someone else's first. You can always create your own later. To make it easier, we have suggested the LP as we know this system works universally and becomes self-implemented by the users.

So, let's get started in summarizing what you should be doing now that you completed the system section of this book. We just discussed how any idea without proper implementation is a wasted thought and the same is with systems. If more people would take the time and energy they waste trying to get others to follow the system and instead focused on using the system themselves, there would be much better results. This is the concept we discussed about being versus telling. When you want a system to be used by others, it is difficult to achieve, but when that system is just who you are, it is near impossible for others who look up to you to avoid using it too.

Planning is a big part of using any system. There is one clear reason why we don't give planning the time it deserves and that is because in the past we have tried planning and it did not go our way. We need to understand that the plan itself means nothing, but planning means everything! If planning is followed by intentional action it is never a waste of time...even if that action is to intentionally choose to take no action at this time.

So, the system we suggest, the LP, is an unbreakable system that when used properly, can handle anyone's life and at any time. This is a big statement, but we have yet to see it not work. The reason is because it is based on natural truths of how humans respond, recall, and refocus. In the beginning we discussed that motivation is not a character trait but rather it is a state of mind, and we all need to be intentional about bringing that motivation mindset out when we need it. The LP puts your thoughts in order so that you can clearly see what steps you need to take as well as let you see your Personal Value Tied to Tasks (PVTT).

The reason the LP is even more valuable is because it can also be used to motivate others. Everything that you learned in these last three sections of the Motivation Formula naturally happens when you and your Motivatee are both using the LP. It is a system that allows both you and them to understand exactly what needs to happen and allows for clear follow through. The LP delivers just a simple conversation.

As you are introducing systems to individuals, we want to make sure that we set two standards. We are all about big goals and dreams but in order to reach that destination, consistency is always better than intensity. We discussed the concept of Bare Ass

Minimum (BAM) which is a valuable tool to have when working with others. This is the lowest standard that will be accepted. This is not something that should be difficult to achieve. BAM is not something that keeps the progress stagnant. BAM should always consist of meaningful small steps in the correct direction to achieve the desired goal. Make BAM attainable because accomplishment and confidence builds momentum in individuals and will allow them to raise their own bar to the level you need at a pace they can handle.

Motivation for everyone is different so we need to make sure whatever it is we are offering is something they are interested in. If the system does not produce results that matter to the motivatee, it will be challenging to keep people using it. If we do not plan, then we have no idea where we are going and even more importantly, where we have been. And if we do not offer the motivatee something that sparks their motivation continuously we are always going to be exerting too much effort motivating others. So, as we develop the system, there is an outcome we are expecting. When we get that outcome, how will we let our motivatee(s) celebrate. For years it has been done by just giving money when something is achieved. It has since been proven that money is not a long-term solution for motivation. So, as we are implementing the system we decided to use, let's make sure we are offering the right Motivation Packages for the individuals using the system. This is a package that is offered so any motivatee can easily connect PVTT. The Motivational Catalysts will determine what to offer them in this package. When we use the catalyst properly, these Motivation Packages can correct the Motivation Synapse between actions and outcomes.

To tie all of this together, it needs to be understood that it is ok to ask for the impossible. When we have strong variables in the motivational formula meaning we know our self, we know "them" and we know our system, we can start going after things we never thought we could do as both an individual and as a team. Most managers just go about giving people a list of what they should do. When you follow this formula, you are not leading others to discover what they should do, but you are giving them a system to do it successfully.

People want to be pushed when they have some confidence that they can handle what is being asked of them. We are asking for a lot and are comfortable to ask for it because we know we give them exactly what they need to stay motivated and achieve the tasks. The key to all of this is to push people, give them the tools they need, and set them up for success.

Part 4 of Motivation Formula - (You + Them) x System = <u>RESULTS</u>

KNOWING THE RESULTS

What would life be like if we knew the results of every action we take? Eventually, life would become a bit boring.

Life is the ultimate game that we get the opportunity to play each day. As much as we wish we could know what was coming, having that element of chance is what makes life worth living. But even with that element of chance, is there a way to have the results be a bit more predictable?

Another name for results is "outcomes." We act and out comes the results. One difference between successful people and unsuccessful people is the way they perceive actions and outcomes.

It's almost like unsuccessful people see an action as the outcome. When the result comes, there is nothing that can now be done. The way they think is simple: "I did this action and got this result." The thought tends to end there. Successful people see results as a data point. "I did this action, which got me this result. Let me see if I can refine the result by refining the action..."

So, when motivating the unmotivated, we can use data from the past to predict results. Knowing as much as you possibly can about the past will allow you to have a better understanding of the future result.

When using a proven system, like the LP, you have a consistent formula to enable you to get the results you want. And you can easily track outcomes and use them as data points.

For you, the reader who has made it this far, the results are not the end here, either; they are a data point. By using the formula we taught you not only will be able to better predict the results, but you will be able to get even more effective results from yourself and your motivatee as time goes on. If you do not like the results, just refine the variables (actions) that cause that result. Instead of spending time worrying about the results, take some time and think about what you can do to get better results.

If you think you have mastered the YOU section yet are not getting the results you want, we need to review and refine what we are doing and how we are going to move forward. You know if you are doing the YOU section right if you are getting what you want out of what you are doing. Wordy I know, but it is true. If you think you know THEM yet you are not getting the results you want, then like stated above it is time to review and refine your action so you can get what you want which is also to help "them" get what they want!

At this point, you have what it takes to be a Motivation All-Star. To me, a Motivational All-Star is able to move people in a positive direction during their lifetime. Basically, they get results through motivation and NOT manipulation. They can be anyone from athletes to politicians to religious leaders. Including someone in this list doesn't mean I agree with everything they did, but I respect their ability to motivate others at the time when they were doing so. The "Five Characteristics of a Motivational All-Star" were created using the common traits of these individuals. This is an evolving list, and we are constantly changing it based on votes by our readers and clients. Feel free to check out our website (www.LifePulseInc.com/MotivationalAllStar) and help vote on who you feel should be on the list as a Motivational All-Star.

When it comes to motivation, we're looking at the following variables in the Motivation Formula:

$$(Motivator + Motivatee) \times System = Results$$

Or

$$(You + Them) \times System = Results$$

- Two parties need to be involved: motivator and motivatee
- A system needs to be used
- The system needs to produce proven results due to the actions of the motivator

The five characteristics of a Motivational All-Star are as follows:

1. **Genuine care for people:** True motivators don't try to manipulate others. Their motivational efforts stem from a genuine desire to make a difference in others' lives for their own good.
2. **Living Proof:** They live what they teach.
3. **Unwavering faith:** Their foundation is nearly unbreakable. They might have gone through a series of experiences that molded them into monuments of motivation.
4. **Patience to do the right thing:** They have an incredible ability to be patient. Remember the section about being "A. P.R.O." and the definition of patience? They bear pain and trials calmly and without complaint, manifesting forbearance under strain, acting without haste or impetuousness, and are steadfast despite opposition.
5. **Simple ideas that are universally applicable:** What matters far more than appearing smart, successful, or wise is communicating profound truths in a simple way.

If you can make sure you have these 5 traits in each task you try to accomplish getting others to follow will be much easier. No matter where they are, if you can do these 5, they will be drawn to you and will be drawn to your leadership.

At this point, you should be able to connect outcome with actions. You can see that if you make this small investment in time and energy in the beginning, you will experience the results you want. There have been many books about having a Growth Mindset and Fixed Mindset. Many unmotivated individuals who are struggling with the synapse between action and outcome see results as the end. That is the Fixed Mindset. The Growth Mindset is where I hope you are now. This is where you can see the results exactly as you should—not seen as the end, but rather as a reference point along the journey toward the results you want.

CHAPTER 32
PLAN YOUR PB&J
Simple but Delicious

It takes far fewer resources to avoid a problem than it does to fix one.

Most of us don't plan because we don't make time for it. Planning just isn't a priority. When we're working with a motivatee, however, we have to invest time in them, which requires planning. When motivating yourself to do this, I've found that it's helpful to think of life in terms of business transactions.

If you were a venture capitalist on the show *Shark Tank* and someone asked for a million dollars to fund their startup, would you want to see their business plan first or would you just take their word that everything will be okay? What if you were building a house? Let's say you meet with a builder, show him a couple of pictures from a magazine, and he quotes you a timeframe and a price. Would you want to see floorplans or architectural drawings before you get started, or would you just assume everything will work out exactly as you want?

The answers to both situations should be obvious, but it's interesting how often we take an entirely different approach to other situations in our life. We launch into action and hope for the best, and we usually end up paying the price for it. Benjamin Franklin supposedly once said: "An ounce of prevention is worth a pound of cure." If we get in the habit of planning our steps before we take them, we'll save quite a bit of time and money in the long run.

The risks of not planning with employees are extremely high. According to a 2017 report by *Training Magazine*, US employee training expenditures were $90.6 billion for the year.[28] Many companies dedicate a full third of their budget to training and development. These costs would likely be much lower if we planned and spent less time retraining.

We are going to have to invest in the people we want to grow. It's been repeatedly proven that investing this time up front also increases the likelihood that an employee will stay with your business for a more extended period of time, decreasing overall training costs that are due to turnover. When we bring a new distributor into one of our sales organizations, we dedicate at least twenty-four hours of one-on-one training to that person. Once we make that large investment up front, they can go on their way. We've found that this drastically decreases the amount of time we need to spend later.

If you want to see a motivatee succeed, you need to do two things:

1. Develop a plan to get them to achieve the desired results.
2. Invest the necessary time to train them so that they can realistically abide by the plan.

When you're considering how to deliver a plan best, break it down into bite-size chunks. Information overload can paralyze a motivatee. Use small amounts with direct wording, and you'll have a tremendous impact. Most people learn by doing rather than just reading or hearing. The last thing you want to do, which is unfortunately the default for many employers, is print off a manual and

---

[28] "2017 Training Industry Report," *Training Magazine*, 2017, http://trainingmag. com/trgmag-article/2017-training-industry-report/.

hand it to the employee. When it comes time to put the plan into action, you should follow what I call the Five-Finger Approach.

1. I personally complete the action, so I know it works.
2. I do it again while they watch/listen so they can see the process in action.
3. We do it together (role-playing) so they can get some hands-on experience.
4. They do it while I watch, listen, and then coach after.
5. They do it on their own, alone, then come and ask any questions they have.

Depending on the process, this could involve a substantial investment in time and resources. However, take whatever the cost of upfront training is and multiply that several times over to get an idea of what your cost will be if the process is not followed.

To show a simple example of how this will work, imagine that I'm teaching a five-year-old how to make a peanut butter and jelly sandwich. The planning part would involve going to the store and getting the ingredients, then setting aside a time when the child is awake, alert, and in a good mood. Once everything is ready, I do the following:

1. I make the PB&J, so I know the process works.
2. I make the PB&J while they watch/listen so they can see the process in action.
3. We make the PB&J together (role-playing) so they can get some hands-on experience.
4. They make the PB&J while I watch, listen, and then coach after.
5. They make a PB&J on their own, alone, then come and ask any questions they have.

Start with a plan, utilize the Five-Finger Approach, and invest the time up front to teach your motivatees well. Do not be short-sighted in this part of the process...it will save you time, money, and frustration in the long run.

CHAPTER 33
CHANGE IS INEVITABLE.
GROWTH IS INTENTIONAL
Choose a Path

Change is inevitable. Growth is intentional.

The 2017 Deloitte "Global Human Capital Trends Report" demonstrated that technology is changing much more rapidly than humans are. It is a massive exponential growth curve that we are all affected by each day. Things are changing and they are changing faster than ever before. Time has never waiting for anyone but now, with this aggressive change and growth, it seems as if time is moving faster than ever before.

There have been three major industrial revolutions in human history, and each has drastically changed humans. The first of these occurred in the 18th century with the invention of the steam engine. This transformed the effects humans could have on the economy, making new inventions like the locomotive possible. The National Bureau of Economic Research states that the expected lifespan at that time was 41 years. (https://www.nber.org/aginghealth/spring06/w11963.html)

Approximately 100 years later, the second industrial revolution occurred. We began to use electricity, the internal combustion engine, radio, the telephone, and the light bulb. These inventions changed life radically. The average human lifespan at this point was 50 years.

Fast-forward another hundred years and the third industrial revolution had started. This was called the digital revolution and began in the 1980s. Our analog world quickly turned into a digital one as inventions like the personal computer and the Internet became prevalent. The average human lifespan at this point was 77 years.

The gaps between these first three revolutions were significant. They were far enough apart that the average human never lived to see more than one of them. However, the speed of progress is accelerating. In 2016, the World Economic Forum announced our movement into a fourth era of industrialization by naming the theme of their annual meeting "Mastering the Fourth Industrial Revolution." As technology continues to develop, we are advancing beyond digital and moving into the realm of the virtual. Artificial intelligence is becoming a reality, and we can interact with holograms. If the human lifespan continues to follow the trend, we can expect the number of people who live longer than 100 years to increase steadily.

The term "disruptors" is becoming more common because "revolution" is something that takes an extended period. Change is happening so rapidly that even the old word for flipping the world on its head, *revolution*, isn't sufficient to describe it. As the amount of time between disruptors decreases, the average human lifespan is simultaneously increasing. The effects of that are profound.

At no other time in human history has a person lived through more than one industrial revolution. There was plenty of time to adapt slowly. Today, many people who lived through the last industrial revolution are now in their prime working years for the current one. And the gaps are only getting smaller. Change is inevitable. Whether we choose to adapt and thrive is up to us.

Therefore, the LP system is so important. It aligns with how our brain naturally works and streamlines how we operate. The LP system possesses the perfect balance of structure and flexibility needed to withstand all the things we experience in life. Organization and systems have always been important, but we are entering a period in human history where they've become vital. Having a system in place to guide you through these technological transformations is critical.

Change must be part of our plan and strategy—for ourselves and our motivatees. The biggest issues we deal with in nearly every company we work with is the inability to manage change, positive or negative. By the time you are reading this book, the stats about the speed of change will likely be outdated. We need to use systems like the LP, which are as flexible as life needs to be, while having the structure to get things done. We need to have systems in place that give us the margin we need. We need to have a plan to be able to embrace the change that is coming, because no matter how hard you try to stay put, change will happen with or without you.

Plan for change in everything you do. The best way to do this, as you've read in earlier chapters, is to add a margin in all the tasks you are accomplishing and plan for the possible outcomes.

The amount of change we are experiencing today is like the 2.4-mile river swim I did as part of the Ironman. I knew it was coming, I prepared for it, and I succeeded. If I had not oriented myself to the challenges I knew were ahead, I likely wouldn't have survived.

In the same way, we need to be prepared for the inevitability of change. If you choose not to use the LP system, make sure you're implementing something with enough buoyancy to keep you afloat.

CHAPTER 34
HOW DOES THE STORY END?
Results May Vary

Thank you for reading this book. We discussed what happened at the lowest point of my life, and it wasn't pretty. What I want you to know is that my "Heartbeat" time was just a blip, and I'm grateful to get to live such a fantastic life. As a quick reminder, here's what that time in my life consisted of:

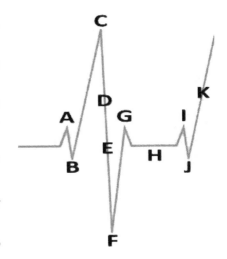

A - Graduated college with a career that was fully set

B - Dreams shattered by an expert's opinion

C - Started first business doing millions in sales and double-digit growth

D - Six-figure embezzlement/mismanagement

E - Given bad bill of health by my doctor

F - Fiancée walks out and no money in bank accounts

G - Romantic getaway to Greece ALONE

H - Plateau of reality

I - Slight excitement with newfound freedom

J - Reality breaking me again

K - Upward tick after developing the Life Pulse system

I met Maria in 2014 while volunteering at Eagle University. I immediately knew that I wanted to marry her, although I had no idea how that would play out. I had just gone through a rollercoaster from hell, and she was in a serious relationship. My self-confidence was shot. At that point, I didn't think I deserved even being on a stage to talk to students.

As I have come to learn, the timing was perfect, as it always is, even if I couldn't see it at the time. If everything hadn't happened just like it did, I wouldn't be writing this book, let alone living the life I am. We had some setbacks early on, but Maria likes to refer to those as "setups" instead. They created the foundation for where we are now.

At first sight, it was obvious that Maria is gorgeous, but the more I got to know her, the more I saw that who she is on the inside is even more attractive and impressive. She's unlike anyone else I've ever met. She is filled with love and passion. Her morals and ethics are unparalleled. She genuinely desires to help others who are in need. She's selfless, wildly intelligent, unbelievably capable, and an amazing wife and mother to our kids. I married up in every sense of the term.

At the end of 2014, going into 2015, I decided to pick a single word that would be my theme for the year. Since this time, each year I select one word each year and I also advise all of my clients to do the same thing. Just to give you some context of what happened in the short years to come from the hardest point in my life, my "heartbeat". By following what was taught in this book, we received the following results as just some of the success. Here is each work for the next 3 years:

Movement

- Engaged to the love of my life
- Transitioned business from retail to wholesale and expanded internationally
- The first print of LP
- Purchased a new home

Optimal

- Married Maria
- Completed an Ironman
- Baptized
  Community

- Moved into a new home
- Natalie was born
- Spoke for the first time professionally

The worst part of my life lasted only a few months, and that brief time of pain set me up for continuous years of absolute bliss. One of the primary themes of this book is connection. We're made to work with others. We're creatures who need community to feel whole. We weren't made to be alone, and motivation doesn't occur in a vacuum. It is often the interaction between two people that spurs everything.

Whether you're motivating someone else or are currently being motivated by another, the process is the same. You might be at a high or low point in life, but the steps don't change. The system works, and it can change your life.

So how does it all end? I have no clue. The story is still being written. I do know that in order to motivate anyone, I need to make sure I'm the best version of myself. One of the ways I do that is to take the necessary time to take care of myself and ensure that I invest in the people I care about. I take time to understand them, put good systems in place, and achieve the results I want.

The formula works 100 percent of the time. It is our responsibility to do everything we can to manage the variables in order to live the life of our dreams—a life of fulfillment, connection, and enjoyment. Ask yourself what part of the formula needs your attention. Work on yourself, help others, and nothing is out of your reach.

RESULTS - Putting the Pieces Together – Post Read

(You + Them) x System = <u>RESULTS</u>

Here is where we get to tie it all up and put it together. The results are what we are all looking to attain, achieve, or reach. The very first part of the book takes you through how to understand motivation. Some of you have had particularly good examples of motivators in your life. You were able to see what it takes to be a good motivator and therefore, it has been easier for you to motivate others. Most of us though, have seen many poor examples of people who should have been motivators who seemed to be more of manipulators in our lives and the lives of others.

Once you have gone through the first section that explains what motivation truly is and how to process our thoughts around motivation, only then can we dive into the act of effectively motivating others.

Out of all the sections in this book that we may have found helpful, we need to stay consistently focused on fine tuning ourselves. Constantly growing and becoming a better version of ourselves is key, the second this stops we will start to lose credibility with those we try to motivate.

Now that we have processed what it takes to get the results or outcomes we desire, it's critical to look back at this statement made in the beginning of the book:

"Well, you now have the simple answer to why people are unmotivated and what to do to motivate the unmotivated. But remember, knowledge is worthless without application. In this book, you will find individual sections

that provide simple strategies for you to use in order to implement this knowledge in your life and relationships."

I told you what you needed to do in the first chapter. As you went through this book, in whatever order you did, you were able to read more about the "how" for each variable of the formula.

The information in this book, although hopefully enjoyable to read, was written so that you could act in these areas of your own formula. This is now the time for you to experience the value of this content. Use it, share it, and most importantly start living by it.

Do not forget to come back to this content and review it I suggest clients to take each chapter, and once a week, take a look at how they are doing in each area. Just taking a second to read the title and focus on that variable for the week helps. You will continue to see result you and your motivatee desire.

If you like the content and philosophy behind this book, then that is the easiest way to know if you would be a good fit for us as a client and if you would be a good fit for you as a coach/consultant. Feel free to reach out directly to our team and we can find ways to help if you have any questions. If you do not like the content or philosophy of this book, then I am impressed you have powered through it to the end.

The results that you want are based on the life that you want to live. This is your decision and needs your direction. That is a lot of responsibility and a scary next step. I can tell you that the more prepared I am, the easier that next step always is. So, once you finish this book, here is the challenge I have for you.

Create a plan on how you are going to implement your plan. This is what we call your Motivation Map. This will guide you to be the best motivator you can be. Take the chapter of this book that you would like to implement, select the week of the year that you would like to "practice" this concept.

Here is what you need to do during the week to make it worth your time. Each day, I want you to see this topic. Some people write it on their mirror with a dry erase marker. Others put it on the screens they look at regularly. I do not care where you put it but just review it each day. At the beginning of the week, I want you to re-read that chapter quickly. Just to refresh yourself. And then finally, I want you to create a plan for the week on places you can implement what was taught.

This may seem like overkill, but I want to make sure I am getting the results, so I am willing to take the actions needed. If you do this, you will be more motivated yourself and those around you will rise to a higher level.

So, remember, motivation is not a character trait, it is a state of mind. You can achieve predictable results as long you are managing each variable effectively. Most would say that THEM is the variable that is more difficult to predict but I can tell you, in the majority of the cases of clients we work with, the issue lies somewhere in the system they are using, and the person doing the motivating. Let's make sure we have all the variables managed properly so we can sit back, relax, and enjoy experiencing the results we all desire.

ABOUT THE AUTHOR

Over the last decade, Matt has tested, developed, and helped thousands of others implement an effective and easy to duplicate system that will help you build an unbreakable foundation for your life as well as motivate even the most unmotivated individuals in your life. These techniques, in formats such as keynotes, workshops, and individual coaching, have been taught and implemented in organizations of all industries and sizes. From Google headquarters and Twitter to the United States Airforce and professional organizations all around the world. Matt has been able to teach these systems to thousands of individuals along with his team at Life Pulse, Inc. Using these concepts Matt has been able to do the following:

- Build his first $1,000,000 business by the age of 25
- Travel all over the world teaching top executives how to build an unbreakable foundation and sustainably motivate others.
- See continued success for thousands of individuals who have applied these systems to their lives and businesses.

With over 10 years and 10,000 hours of studying, using, and teaching these concepts, Matt is considered to be an expert on teaching individuals how to build an unbreakable foundation for themselves as well as their organization, along with how to properly manage motivation.

Along with speaking and coaching, Matt is also an author, featured columnist, and sought-after expert in the field of motivating others. With all the success Matt has experienced, most importantly, Matt is happily married to his wife and business partner (Maria) with two amazing kids (Natalie & Zach). The drive behind Matt is his obsession to make sure no person's potential is wasted and that each person he comes in contact with, if they want, is able to experience their maximum level of success.

Contact us: info@LifePulseInc.com
Website: www.LifePulseInc.com
Follow on Social: @LifePulseInc